PRAISE FOR *DO YOUR CHILDREN BELIEVE?*

"My hope and prayer is that this book will have the same impact on your family as it has had on ours. May it draw your family closer to God and each other for generations to come."

—WANDA CHATMON
WIFE

"Men love a challenge. They become animated talking about leading their team in scoring, leading their company in sales, or reaching the top of their profession and the corner office. But talk about the goal of leading every one of their children to love God with all their hearts, and the room goes silent. Terence Chatmon has written about the leadership that matters most. I encourage you to read it!"

—RICHARD BLACKABY
AUTHOR, *EXPERIENCING GOD AT HOME*

"Who hasn't struggled with how to successfully pass on his faith in Christ to his children? Terence Chatmon provides a powerful path through his own struggles to blossom his hope for his children into reality. If you want practical and authentic wisdom that will guide you to achieve the legacy of your life—your children becoming committed disciples—then Terence's new book is waiting for you!"

—BRUCE WILKINSON
PRESIDENT, TEACH EVERY NATION

"Seven years ago we embarked on a journey as a family that would change my life forever. My dad's starting of a spiritual family plan challenged me to grow deeper in my faith, offered a connection with family, and highlighted the importance of prioritizing what we valued most. Our family relationships are changed because of his hard work, passion, and vision. But most important, our strengthened relationship with God is our rock and foundation."

"Terence has developed a resource that takes the mystery out of developing a family plan. As a leader in our church, he and Wanda have been leading many of our young families through this process, giving them the tools necessary to lead their families. You will find the principles and practices of this great resource extremely helpful."

—RANDY POPE
SENIOR PASTOR, PERIMETER CHURCH

"As parents we want the best for our children, and we strive to leave them an inheritance and words of wisdom to live by; however, I have come to learn that the greatest gift we could ever leave our children is a blueprint on how to build a personal relationship with God. My children know God today because my father took the time to make sure his children knew God and read the Word of God."

—KENITA LEWIS
DAUGHTER

"*Do Your Children Believe?* is timely, highly readable, insightful, and encouraging. I am proud to call Terence my friend and look forward to sharing his book with others."

—RICHARD "DICK" FLAIG
CONSULTANT AND FORMER SVP, THE COCA-COLA COMPANY

"As a parent I have realized that the best thing I can give my son is knowledge of the truth and Christ. Charting has helped me to grow in my personal faith and walk with Christ. It is also equipping me to plant little seeds in my toddler and set a foundation for him as he grows. He may not understand much yet, but he knows who made him, loves him, and protects him."

—SHANNON CHATMON
DAUGHTER-IN-LAW

"This book illustrates where deep parental desire meets workable design, where timid inadequacy meets Christ's sufficiency. Wanda and Terence have lived out their faith in the home, with their children. They are witnessing transformation firsthand and now desire to bless many more with a proven step-by-step plan to raise children in the Lord. Praying the Lord moves to place this book in the lives of *many* families."

—HOWARD DAYTON
FOUNDER, COMPASS: FINANCES GOD'S WAY

"My friend Terence Chatmon is a substantive, practical, gracious, caring leader who has written a great book that is just like the man. This book can change your life as a parent and subsequently change your children's lives. What better legacy is there?"

—DR. RON JENSON
AMERICA'S LIFE COACH

"This book is a gift to Christian families. I pray God uses it and Terence to make a difference in passing the faith from generation to generation."

—DAWN SWABE-ELLIS, MD
PEDIATRICIAN

"As the grandmother of seven, living in a post-Christian culture, I believe the need to leave a spiritual legacy for the next generation has taken on a whole new meaning. It's a matter of spiritual life or death. This tool in the hands of families has the potential to impact them and our society for generations to come."

—DELORES ROSE
FAMILY PLANNING WORKSHOP PARTICIPANT

"As the father of four adult children who are starting their own families, I can easily affirm that *Do Your Children Believe?* by Terence Chatmon is a highly needed resource.

While I am thankful that all of our children and their spouses are followers of Christ, I have become acutely aware that the process of parenting does not end when your children leave home. Rather, the process of mentoring and providing counsel continues. Fortunately, Terence provides the vision, structure, and encouragement needed to continue on the path of providing spiritual instruction to your family, even as you move into the next stage of solidifying your family's legacy."

—PAUL WHITE, PHD
PSYCHOLOGIST, AUTHOR, AND PRESIDENT, APPRECIATION AT WORK

"Terence gives us his best leadership experience in this book and encourages us to live a life with no regret as he lays out his plan to be the spiritual leader of his family, as a follower of Jesus, and leave that legacy to his children and grandchildren. We are called to do nothing less with our families. It's all about Jesus and our love for Him and our families. The time is now!"

—JIM WHITE
DELAP LLP

"The book title alone is enough of a starting point to become intentional about building a family legacy of faith. We spend way too much time building legacies of skills or looks or wealth. Terence sticks his finger into the obvious tear in the fabric and tells us how to start repairing it."

—MARIAN NORONHA
PRESIDENT, TURBOCAM INTERNATIONAL

"During a time of confusion about my faith, due to some of the hard truths in our family Bible studies, the weekly calls kept me close to God. Without the constant guidance and support of the family devotional call, I would have drifted further away from God, but that's the beauty of learning within a family structure in a safe environment. The constant hearing of the truth re-trains the heart and refuels the Holy Spirit, bringing you back to the love of the Father. You can question, work through, and come out on the other side as a family feeling much closer to each other and the Lord. My family has been forever changed because the Word provides death to self and rebirth to a whole new way of walking through this life together as a family."

—TORRY CHATMON
SON

"Terence Chatmon is a walking example of open commitment to leading his family's succeeding generations into an abiding relationship with the Lord. He talks regularly of his heart-felt burden to extend genuine belief in Christ and the authority of the Word of God to the next generation of children who are budding within his own lineage. He personally and professionally mentors young men in the ways of 'working as unto the Lord.' Writing a book and walking out what is written can be two separate things, but in the case of Terence Chatmon, his talk and walk are the same. He illustrates with his life how an individual can demonstrate the cascading priorities of God and family ahead of all else."

—WAYNE ODOM
EXECUTIVE AMBASSADOR, IN TOUCH MINISTRIES

"Terence Chatmon's *Do Your Children Believe?* provides a powerful blueprint to impact a generation and create our families' legacies."

—NICHOLAS V. LEONE III
CEO AND AUTHOR, THE PRINCIPLES SERIES

DO YOUR CHILDREN
BELIEVE?

DO YOUR CHILDREN BELIEVE?

BECOMING INTENTIONAL ABOUT YOUR FAMILY'S FAITH AND SPIRITUAL LEGACY

TERENCE CHATMON

W PUBLISHING GROUP

AN IMPRINT OF THOMAS NELSON

Published in Nashville, Tennessee, by W Publishing Group, an imprint of Thomas Nelson.

Published in association with the literary agency of Wolgemuth & Associates, Inc.

Thomas Nelson titles may be purchased in bulk for educational, business, fundraising, or sales promotional use. For information, please e-mail SpecialMarkets@ ThomasNelson.com.

Library of Congress Cataloging-in-Publication Data

Names: Chatmon, Terence, 1959– author.
Title: Do your children believe?: becoming intentional about your family's faith and spiritual legacy / Terence Chatmon.
Description: Nashville, Tennessee: W Publishing Group, an imprint of Thomas Nelson, [2017]
Identifiers: LCCN 2016013586 | ISBN 9780718078263 (trade paper)
Subjects: LCSH: Christian education of children. | Christian education—Home training.
Classification: LCC BV1475.3 .C43 2017 | DDC 248.8/45—dc23
LC record available at https://lccn.loc.gov/2016013586

Printed in the United States of America

17 18 19 20 21 LSC 6 5 4 3 2 1

*To my dear wife, Wanda, who has been my
partner and support on the journey. And to my
children, who continue to be our discipleship
group as we live out this journey together.*

*To Perimeter Church leadership, who challenged
and prepared me along the way for something so
bold that it would fail unless God was in it.*

*To all loving parents who read this book and follow its
biblical principles to train and instruct your children
in the Lord. You are leaving a spiritual legacy for
this lifetime and beyond. Continue to be intentional
through the journey, remembering that the struggle
strengthens our character, perseverance, and hope.*

Bring them up in the training and
instruction of the Lord.
—Ephesians 6:4

CONTENTS

Foreword by Steve Green xiii

PART I: THE CALLING

1 Better Answers to Good Questions 3

2 Making It Personal 17

3 Steps in the Right Direction 31

PART II: THE PLAN

4 From Daunting to Doable 47

5 Up and Down the Family Tree 61
  Step 1: Discover Your Spiritual Heritage

6 The Story of Your Life 75
  Step 2: Articulate Your Testimony

7 Who? What? How? 89
  Step 3: Define Your Values, Your Vision, Your Mission

8 Intentions in Action 107
  Step 4: Set Your Goals

CONTENTS

9 Fun for All Ages 121
Step 5: Personalize Your Plan to Fit All Your Children

10 Who Do You Know Who Needs Jesus? 135
Step 6: Adopt a Family Prayer Focus

11 Live It Like You Mean It 149
Step 7: Draft Your Family Covenant

12 Momentum-Building Moments 159

PART III: THE PURSUIT

13 Sufficient to the Struggle 175

14 Legacy 185

Appendix A: Generational Spiritual Development Plan . . . 195

Appendix B: Sample Devotional Plan 201

About the Author 207

FOREWORD

I was blessed to be born into a family where Christ was truly the center—not only of our home but of everything we did. We were shown each day, both by word and example, that we'd been put on this earth for a reason: to love and serve the Lord Jesus.

I have seen the difference it makes when parents are genuinely invested in their children's faith. I have seen how it filters out into all of life and filters down to the next generation. I have seen how it sharpens a child's identity, focuses a son's mind, influences a daughter's decisions, and opens up for them a whole world of God-blessed, God-inspired opportunities, big and small.

Home is where it happens. Family is where it starts.

So count me as being fully on board with the message of my friend Terence Chatmon and this book. He and I first connected as businessmen but soon bonded as brothers in Christ. I have heard the excitement in his voice when we have talked about his passion for equipping parents, not only to *raise* their children but actually to *disciple* them in the Word. He would be the first to tell you that he didn't feel up to this task with his kids. (None of us do.) Nor did he start taking it seriously as early in their lives as he would have wished. (Most of us don't.) But what other endeavor could possibly be more deserving of our time, prayer, and effort than this primary responsibility as parents . . . with the people we love more than anyone else in the world?

I have always been impressed with the work Terence does through Fellowship of Companies for Christ International (FCCI), providing tools and training for business leaders all over the world, helping them run their companies for Christ with a keen eye for generational impact. I am grateful as well for his support of initiatives such as the Museum of the Bible in Washington, DC. He has proven himself to me as a man of vision and cultural change. But I believe the impact of his book, if read and practiced, can be transformational. Moms and dads, modeling Christ in our homes—there's the foundation for a revitalized society.

God's best for you starts with you giving your family the priority He calls for. Terence will inspire and challenge you through his journey in that pursuit. The rewards for you and your family are both temporal and eternal. What could be better than that?

—Steve Green

President, Hobby Lobby

PART I

THE CALLING

CHAPTER 1

BETTER ANSWERS TO GOOD QUESTIONS

I 've never met a man of faith who didn't want to be the spiritual leader in his home. He may not have known whether he could *do* it, may not have seen how he could possibly make *time* for it, but it's something he knows he should do. And wishes he was doing.

At the same time, I've rarely, if ever, met a woman of faith who wasn't dying for her husband to ascend to that role. And if he won't, or if he isn't there to do it, she realizes *she's* going to need to be that for her children. Whatever it takes. It's that important.

Believing parents know their kids need a strong foundation of faith, and they want to be able to give it to them.

So you'd think with this much consensus there wouldn't be a neighborhood in America where at some point in the evening, or at least at some point in the week, half the families weren't huddled together over the Scriptures, holding hands in prayer, kicked back in serious spiritual conversation, or making plans for their next big ministry project over the weekend or during the summer.

Yet even with such honest, across-the-board desire—on *everyone's* part—the hard truth remains that fewer than 10 percent of Christian families ever really engage with one another for the express purpose of encouraging or informing their growing faith. And not *1 percent* could show you any kind of written plan that even briefly describes the spiritual direction they're praying for and working toward together.[1]

If ever there was a math equation that didn't make sense or add up, it's *that* one.

And it has me wondering *why*. Not that for twenty years of married life I wasn't square in the middle of the 99.9 percenters. Despite having been a prominent business executive with three of the most recognizable companies in the world (Citibank, Coca-Cola, and Johnson & Johnson), despite being an elder at one of the largest churches in the greater Atlanta area, despite being confident in my abilities to lead a well-constructed Bible study for any group of people on any given Sunday, I was admittedly failing—and failing miserably—as the spiritual leader in my home. I was succeeding just about everywhere in life I could succeed, except for the one place where I was truly irreplaceable. I was proving to be inept and inadequate at the only job where

---

1 "Assessment of Church Families" (Colorado Springs, CO: Constituent Insights for Focus on the Family, 2007), 6–7. See also Barna, Research: Family & Kids, "Parents Accept Responsibility for Their Child's Spiritual Development but Struggle with Effectiveness," May 6, 2003, https://www.barna.com/research/parents-accept-responsibility-for-their-childs-spiritual-development-but-struggle-with-effectiveness; Timothy Paul Jones, "Family Ministry: Doing Less So That Parents Can Do More," Timothy Paul Jones (blog), October 21, 2013, http://www.timothypauljones.com/family-ministry-doing-less-so-that-parents-can-do-more.

no one else could come along to bail me out or fill in for me if things went south.

But something did come along to reverse this inverted picture of what a godly family man was supposed to be. And if you are willing to join me for a little while, I think you'll see something that might be helpful for you as well.

One chilly December weekend, my wife, Wanda, and I were away from home, off on an anniversary trip to the north Georgia mountains. We try to do these brief getaways every year, but this one was particularly special—we were celebrating fifteen years together in marriage. The peace and quiet gave us time to talk without interruption about both the past and the future, our memories and our dreams. It was wonderful. I was loving every minute of it. Until . . .

Being the business leader that I am—and Wanda being the thoughtful woman that she is—we already had actually planned to spend a portion of our weekend reflecting on three specific questions in terms of our lives together, especially as they related to our children and family: (1) *Where have we been?* (2) *Where are we?* and (3) *Where are we going?* Call it a romance-buster if you like, but Wanda and I have found that taking the time to intentionally talk about our relationship and our family always draws us closer and enhances our marriage. We had even written out some notes to ourselves beforehand—a working list of our personal hopes, fears, and observations. We didn't want to overlook anything while we had each other's full attention and were thinking big-picture about our marriage, our family, our life, our future.

Back and forth we went—an unhurried rekindling of the

vows we'd made more than a decade earlier. Real life in real time. Some of it rich and full; some of it competing, confusing, and highly challenging because any time you have children, as you know, you have worries and concerns. Even if they're good kids—as ours were—even if they're steady in church, strong in character, staying out of trouble—life is still working against them all the time. And it's working simultaneously against our focused attention as parents on what we truly need to be for our children.

Wanda, astute as ever, had really been picking up on this. In addition to being hard at work managing the everyday, present demands of our home and family, she'd already begun widening her field of vision to notice some treacherous ground down the road, much sooner than I'd begun to see it. She was grateful for how well our kids were doing and proud of who they were growing up to be. But she was beginning to ache in advance for the kinds of settings and scenarios they were fast approaching, times when Sunday school answers wouldn't cut it any longer, when their faith would need to be theirs, not just an extension of ours, when the questions and confrontations would be consistently bigger and the stakes higher than any of the ones they'd faced until then.

"I just wonder, Terence," she asked me that December day around the fire, "do you think they're really prepared to defend their faith, say, in a college environment?"

Good question. Hearing it stated so bluntly like that, I admit the sudden notion did frighten me as well. We'd done a decent job, I thought, of teaching our kids honesty and commitment and personal responsibility. How to manage their time, their money. I felt pretty good about all that. But my bride was right.

I couldn't sit there and answer her with any firm level of confidence that yes, our children were up to the task of a professor with an agenda or to the needling questions of a roommate with serious, cynical doubts about God's existence.

This was indeed a problem. Something we really ought to be thinking about. In fact, that's exactly how I answered her:

"What do you think we ought to do about it?"

Pause here for a pregnant moment of silence—because next came the one question that not only challenged my whole perception of myself as a parent but, over the course of years, also has led to a radical change in our family's life and even to the writing of this book. Throughout the many days since, my wife's question has moved me from being a man consumed by my work and its weekly timetable into a man who's driven instead by what the generations of our family will look like a hundred years from now. No longer am I at a loss for words about the true state of my children's relationship with God, having no real clue where they stand in their grasp of biblical truth and their love for walking with Him. And it's all because of one question, perfectly timed—a question that sliced through the compulsive fog of my career-driven significance, forcing me to determine in that moment whom I was going to be as a man.

"What do you think we ought to do about it?" I'd said to her—my reflex response, spoken with all the sheepish instinct of the typically passive husband and father. Wanda's comeback, however, was much better than mine. It went something like this:

"We?

"No.

"What are *you* going to do about it?"

I (and we) have never been quite the same since.

A TALE OF TWO GENERATIONS

Writing a book like this is difficult, not because I'm dealing with any shortage of passion on the subject or I'm unclear about what to say but because I realize I'm issuing a challenge that seems nearly impossible to many people. It certainly did to me.

Your reaction to what I'm about to say on family discipleship—despite a keen interest and desire on your part to grow in this area, as well as in your spiritual leadership at home—could easily fall victim to discouragement or to a curt, overwhelmed dismissal. We humans are nothing if not creatures of habit. The path of least resistance is almost always the path we've been the most comfortable taking. We're old hands at dropping back and punting. We're quick to look at what others are apparently doing well and automatically conclude, hey, we're not anything like *them*. We sure can't do it like *they* do it.

You may already be sitting there right now, thinking, *He obviously doesn't have the same challenges or set of circumstances I do. Sounds good on paper, I guess, but it'll never fly here. Not with me. Not with us.*

I get that.

The makeup of your family may seem like a source of complication. You may be the parent or grandparent, for instance, to children of various ages, with varying temperaments and experiences—toddlers to teenagers in different stages of life and with different attention spans. Your kids may even be grown, with schedules and interests that are hardly under your control anymore. You may be a single parent, forced into this role through unfortunate circumstances you never intended or saw coming. And you're thinking, *Come on, Terence, I'm barely making it work as it is.*

In addition, regardless of the makeup of your family, your background and personal history may come with its own built-in excuses for considering yourself disqualified from pressing forward: lack of knowledge, lack of time, and lack of the kind of track record that gives your voice much influence, authority, and credibility at home. The potential barriers to success can be large and layered. You look around, note the land mines, and decide you're better off just backing away from the responsibility, hoping your kids can somehow figure out all this stuff without you. I get that too.

But here's how I'd like to begin our discussion. The following example cuts across all demographics and obstacles, presenting a predicament that's common to each of us. It's a looming crisis that remains as relevant today as it did four thousand years ago in the history of God's people.

Among all the heroes of the Bible, few can match the sterling example and reputation of Joshua—the Old Testament leader of Israel after the death of Moses; a stout warrior of deep conviction, valor, and principle; a courageous visionary who brought back a daring minority report on the desirability of the promised land, and then later led the entire nation in laying claim to it by conquering a vast number of established, enemy armies. Joshua—whose given name and legacy proved semi-prophetic of Jesus, the One who would walk that very land of promise two millennia later—was a man among men, a spiritual giant of his time.

All of which makes the biblical report of Joshua's death in Judges 2 and its immediate aftermath so noticeably surprising and distressing. Joshua, "the servant of the LORD" (v. 8), died and was buried in the hill country of Canaan, as were all his contemporaries in the days and years that followed. "That whole generation," the Bible says, in language that sounds very King James in tone, had been "gathered to their ancestors." But then the writer of the book of Judges added this disheartening observation: "another generation grew up who knew neither the LORD nor what he had done for Israel" (v. 10).

The very next generation.

They were already starting to forget.

Let that dire, descriptive statement settle on you for just a minute.

Those who had grown up during the years when Joshua and his fellow leaders had shepherded their homes and nation were now adults and parents themselves, raising the next generation of God's people. According to God's Word, the prevailing pattern at play at that moment in Israel's history was of families and children who hadn't been taught, who couldn't remember, who didn't themselves possess a personal, intimate knowledge of the God who had made them distinctive as a nation. Shocking, isn't it?

One generation, twenty years, give or take. Fresh on the heels of the Jordan River crossing, the fall of Jericho, the hard lessons of their defeat at Ai.

Joshua, you'll recall, in his farewell sermon had admonished the people with what's now a famous challenge: "Choose for yourselves this day whom you will serve, whether the gods your ancestors served beyond the Euphrates, or the gods of the Amorites, in whose land you are living. But as for me and my household, we will serve the LORD" (Josh. 24:15). They answered his appeal that day with a unanimous rally cry: "Far be it from us to forsake the LORD to serve other gods! . . . We will serve the LORD our God and obey him" (vv. 16, 24). In celebration, Joshua ordered that a large stone be set up as a permanent memorial of this historic moment. He declared the monument a *witness* to the promises they had made, as well as a *warning* against failing to follow through on their covenant with God and with one another.

Yet, after a few more cycles of the earth around the sun, the world these ancient people inhabited became a place where they and their children—to repeat the leaden testimony of Judges 2:10—"knew neither the LORD nor what he had done for Israel."

This verse just nails me. Even with an up-close understanding of myself and my own heart, even with an acute awareness for how fickle we humans can be by nature, this dramatic turnaround in the people's zeal and devotion strikes me as incredible. It's unthinkable. So fast. So precipitous. So deep a dive into disinterest, disbelief, and (as the woeful accounts from the book of Judges would go on to describe) the long-term decay of their once-mighty nation. Years of suffering, death, and oppression would follow—*snap!* Just like that—as if their miraculous, redeeming, overpowering history with God had never happened.

Unbelievable.

I take this observation from Scripture as a grave, cautionary tale. Tell me, in fact, that we're not seeing some of these same conditions in the age in which we live. I won't bore you with a bunch of statistics; you probably know or can deduce many of them from what you've seen, heard, and, perhaps, personally experienced. You know, for example, the extent to which destruction and disharmony exist in the modern family—and how much even churchgoing Christian families possess in common with families who barely claim to know God at all. But more important—and more personally—you know what's almost sure to happen if your children venture into young adulthood and beyond without developing a vibrant, thriving relationship with Christ, without being discipled by parents in a loving home environment, and without discovering through prayer and firsthand experience what their God is truly capable of, the work He has done and can still very much do.

I'm not talking about whether your children have professed belief in Christ or been baptized, officially marking themselves as Christians, as church members. I'm talking about kids who deeply know the Word, kids who are confident in articulating the basis for their faith, kids who are active in synthesizing their biblical understanding with the kinds of lifestyles they lead and the heart for service and servanthood they embody.

If you want to see those kinds of kids develop from the seats around your table, through the offhand, ongoing, organic living out of godly truth in your home, I'm here with what I *know* from experience to be a proven, biblical plan for putting this enormous task into God's hands and watching His sufficiency take over with astounding effect.

I'm here to help you answer the question, "What are *you* going to do about it?"

LEGACY BOUND

I'm convinced that you, like most parents, want to do the right thing. You want your kids to grow spiritually, mature in the faith, and (as the apostle Peter said) be able to "give an answer to everyone who asks you to give the reason for the hope that you have" (1 Peter 3:15). As a dad, I wanted those things, too, not only for my children but also for me. I wanted to grow and mature—all of us, all together.

One problem: I didn't know how to make that happen.

And most likely that's you. You want it. You've *always* wanted it. But you've just never really known how to go about it. You haven't known where to start. Neither did I. It sounds too hard, too far above us. Borderline impossible.

The plan I'm going to share with you in this book is, I admit, challenging. Anything that's worthwhile always is. But at the same time—and I'm not just saying this to oversell you and keep you hooked on the line here—it's also very easy once you get going.

You don't need to be a theological expert. You don't need to complete a thorough curriculum of study courses to gear up and get ready for it. Nor should you feel pressure to cram a whole lifetime's worth of experiences into whatever number of years remain while your children are still under your roof. It's bigger, broader, and more far-reaching than that. The plan I'll be giving you is not a step-by-step manual to be followed to the letter, right down the line. Instead, it's something, with God's help, you'll be able to develop in a way that uniquely fits your family—now and, hopefully, for many years to come.

Bottom line: this is not about completing a Bible study, following a prescription, or checking an item off your to-do list. Ultimately, this is about *legacy*.

More than anything else in my life, as a result of the journey God has led us on these past fifteen years or so, *legacy* is what wakes me up in the morning. Sure, I'm currently the president and CEO of a major nonprofit organization with strategic outreaches in the marketplace, working with some of today's finest business leaders, not only in America but in more than a hundred countries around the world. I'm devoted to this work, and I give it my very best every day. I also remain actively involved in our local church, and I love its people and ministries with all my heart. I take my community responsibilities seriously and participate in a number of groups that share my values and interests.

But none of these endeavors rival the priority I feel for leaving a legacy of faith for my children, my grandchildren, and the future generations of our family that will keep expanding and spiraling into the future until Jesus comes—when He welcomes His *entire* family into the eternal dwelling He's preparing for us even now.

That's why, if all you've been able to see in your mind's eye as you've been reading so far is some stereotypical, methodical process of family worship, I want to show you in this first chapter that is not what I'm talking about. It's a whole-life, wholehearted approach that knows no boundaries of possibilities. And the resulting joy you're going to experience, I promise you, is off-the-charts fulfilling.

Our three children cover a gamut of ages, from their twenties to their thirties. Two are married, and each leads an active, busy life. Yet every other Sunday evening, by shared consent—as recently as last week and as soon again as next week—our combined families get together by phone to spend a good hour or more in devotions, prayer, and faith-building with one another. Every year we together work out our spiritual goals, deciding as a group what we want to accomplish. I hope, with the strength

God gives me, to be enjoying these times with my children (and their children) for as long as I'm alive.

I'm not finished being their father just because they're out of the house. I'm not done providing active, hands-on, in-person spiritual leadership to my family.

They are—this is—my legacy.

I invite you to join me . . . for the glory of God and the yet unknown reach of your family line in His future plans for the kingdom. Like me, you won't do it perfectly. You'll mess up. You'll make mistakes. But God will be who God always is: our Completer, our Provider, our Rescuer, our Guide back home. He will make you an ambassador for His Son, Jesus Christ, in the one place where your influence can be felt like no other. Everything that has made you feel as though you're slogging through your Christian life, just doing stuff to be doing it, is about to be transformed into something completely new and different. As someone who's always wanted to do the right thing as a parent, you now can actually watch it happen, maybe for the first time, with an all-new level of excitement and passion.

And *that*, my friend, is what *you* (and God) are going to do about it.

CHAPTER 2

MAKING IT PERSONAL

Remember when activities that kept people away from church on Sunday included catching up on yard work; relaxing at the lake, whether with a fishing pole or a picnic lunch; pulling an additional shift for the chance to make time-and-a-half or more; and putting in the extra time needed to build that new house? These excuses for church absence, for the most part, were more the rule than the exception and provided a snapshot of people's priorities.

Now it seems whole families have started to regularly miss Sunday worship for big chunks of the year because of weekend soccer tournaments, AAU ball, travel teams, or other kinds of extracurricular activities. I mean, who wouldn't agree the kids are important, right? Being supportive and involved in their lives is a good thing for parents to do, isn't it?

Sure, okay. I hear you. I played a little high school baseball in my time. Couldn't quite get up to ninety on the radar gun, but I did all right. So I know about the value of sports when you're growing up and of parents being there to cheer you on. Sure.

But choices like these—in fact, all the choices we make—are windows on our priorities, even if those priorities compete with and contradict the ones that, deep down, we most want to possess, the ones that stand the best chance of outliving us and truly changing the culture and people around us. So I use these particular examples to show how even good things—catching up on much-needed chores; supporting our kids' activities; working extra hours to provide for the family, pad a college scholarship fund, or pay our dues for a much bigger payout, hopefully, down the line—can trick us into thinking we're choosing the best, that we're choosing wisely.

Problem is, there's only so much room in our lives to accommodate a limited number of priorities. And if we continue crowding out the ones that matter most—the ones that matter most spiritually, the ones that matter most eternally—all these years of noise and activity will one day quiet into a future that's not exactly the one for which we hoped. It will, however, be the one for which we planned. Based on our priorities.

So as I was wrestling with Wanda's question to me about how I intended to get our kids ready to face life with a more active faith and knowledge and trust in Jesus Christ, I came to a staggering conclusion: the priorities I was living by were not capable of pulling that off.

I was being a pretty good dad. Anybody would've told you that. Even with my crazy travel schedule, I always tried to arrange it so I didn't have to miss anyone's baseball or basketball games. Ever. We went to church as a family. The kids were happy with me. My wife was happy with me. I truly adored them and was trying my hardest to make sure they had everything they needed and just about everything they wanted.

But I had abdicated my role of spiritual leadership to Wanda. *She* was the one who was in the Word on a regular basis. *She* was the one with the dynamic prayer life. *She* was the one who was developing our kids spiritually. Not me. And we'd concluded that this dynamic simply wasn't enough. Wouldn't cut it.

So through the course of following up on these newly expressed convictions in our lives, we made a momentous decision: I would focus more of my attention as the spiritual leader of the family. But during our fourth year as owners of several trendy soup-and-sandwich locations, my workload was up, toward eighty or ninety hours per week. (That was bad.) It soon started getting out of hand, with both Wanda and I working in the store; other family members also were working in the store; we were basically serving as the emergency, call-in staff for *every* store. So now, instead of just me being somewhat out of the spiritual loop with my family, I had worked it so that both Wanda *and* I were losing time and focus on our family. We were meeting ourselves coming and going. We were having to call on friends to take our kids to church for us. We were ceding ground that we had hoped to conquer once I was able to be at home with more consistency. Something needed to change.

And the main thing that needed to change was me.

PLAN OF A LIFETIME

I can say, with almost complete confidence, that no matter who you are or where you've been, the first step toward becoming the spiritual leader in your home is to realize you can't do it. Even as you *try* to do it—by leaning more and more on the power of the Holy Spirit—it almost certainly won't happen as long as your priorities remain where they are situated currently.

Please don't let that discourage you. First, anyone who would look down on you for being willing to make this admission is most likely covering for the fact that he is in the same shape as (or a worse shape than) you are. Priority drift and shift is a fairly universal problem for all of us. And second, the changes you may need to make, while perhaps significant and sacrificial (as mine were), don't mean you've been a complete failure up to now or that you need a 100-percent makeover. They just mean you need to recalibrate. You need a more intentional direction. You need focus. You need what all of us need: the determination to make a plan, as well as the courage to do whatever it takes to execute it.

Being the spiritual leader in your home does not require an additional educational degree or set number of Bible study credits. As long as you're a believer in Christ—trusting Him by faith alone in grace alone for the forgiveness of your sins—you can consider yourself the spiritual leader of your home. Right now. Immediate occupancy. You can start today. God has placed you in this position as a parent within your family, entrusting you with one or more members of His creation (your children) to guide and steward them as a gift from His hand. You may not know exactly how to *do* it yet. Few, if any, of us ever do. We all learn and grow and back up and start over again, and we never stop needing to plant our full weight on the power of God to help us. But the job is already yours. You're hired. If you need me to say it with a little more Christian-sounding language, how's this: You are *called* to this task. And there's no time to waste.

But part of the basic equipment you need in preparing to start work is a tweaked set of priorities because some of the old ones—the ones that have kept you from actively accepting this responsibility—have obviously been working against you. So unless you allow those to go by the wayside, or unless you at least drop them down a few rungs, things will just keep going the way they have been. And I don't think that's why you're reading this book.

The first order of business in this noble endeavor is not a plan for how you're going to lead your family spiritually with more mission and purpose. (We'll get to that later.) You'll first need a plan designed to iron out your own mission and purpose. As a person. A vision of where *you* want to go. Spiritually. A hard look at what you're presently doing, what matters most to you, and how much of it is dead weight that you cannot afford to carry around with you any longer—not if you're going to position yourself for real spiritual growth and leadership.

For me, I already had a plan for my life. But my plan had a problem, not for what it contained but for what it didn't contain. My vision and goal were to change the way corporate America was done. My father had drilled into my brothers and me the idea that through business (or sports, if we wanted to go that route), we could exert a sizable amount of force on culture. "Business is what shapes society," he had preached to us, "and whatever shapes society has maximum influence." He taught me that by working my way into leadership and management, along with gaining the commensurate authority to hire and fire people, I could create everyday examples of one of God's first principles: everyone has essential value. And if given the opportunity to put forth the hard work, anyone can realize their potential and transform the world around them.

So, man, I was going for it. Not to land a certain job. Not to make a certain amount of money. Just *to change the way corporate America was done.* From the top. Doing it better. Doing it differently, where needed. Doing it faster. Helping *everybody* who worked for me understand that they possessed essential value and they could both benefit and contribute to society through their God-given abilities. I'd mapped it out, claimed it as my vision, and devoted myself to living it to its fulfillment. Raising up leaders. Inspiring lofty goals. Changing people's lives.

Anything wrong with that? Of course not.

And yet, while caught up in all my impressive, aggressive agendas, I was overlooking the most important objective of all. In trying to change the way corporate America was done, I wasn't changing the way *family* was done. *Christian* family. Not in my house at least. I wasn't leading my family in our faith.

Listen, I'm not telling you to quit your job. I'm not proposing you do anything brazenly radical. I'm not saying you can't be the best at whatever work you've been given the opportunity to do. I'm just asking—that's all I'm really here for, just to ask, just to make some observations and suggestions: Will your priorities, as they're presently arranged, help to make you the kind of person who leaves the greatest possible legacy behind you?

If not, what needs to change?

This, I knew, was where I needed to start. And, I daresay, it's the place where you need to start as well.

BEST PRACTICES

If you don't know the Bible, you really can't be effective at making it come to life for your children. If you don't pray often, you can't really do much more than just talk about prayer in vague, general, impersonal terms. And if you're not devoting some serious time to both the Bible *and* prayer, this means something else is stealing those hours right out from under your nose. It's not just stealing from *you*; it's stealing from your kids, your spouse, your legacy, and generations of faith in which you can already be investing.

You'd be shocked at how quickly, once you dedicate yourself to it, the Lord can start bringing the Scriptures into living color and structure and direction for your life. But you have to want it. You have to open it. You've got to start making it a disciplined, deliberate part of every day.

It might mean you watch only *one* ballgame on Saturday instead of three. It might mean you give your various electronic devices a few hours' rest this week, instead of streaming another show or staying current on what everybody else is doing and watching and laughing about. It might mean getting up at 5:00 a.m., instead of 6:00 a.m., every once in a while and finding out how much God can accomplish and accelerate within you in just sixty minutes' time of prayer and Bible reading.

I knew what it meant for me. And I decided it was worth whatever it cost. I needed to know what my kids needed to know . . . about God, about life. I needed to seek the kind of relationship with Him that I wanted them to experience so I could *show* them it was real, not just talk about it. I wanted the kind of faith that would rub off on them through real interactions together as a family, not through some kind of forced "Bible time." I wanted to model genuine love for God, not boring legalities. Genuine love for others, not guilty obligations.

So I set off on a journey to find all of that.

And the Lord, in quick answer to my prayer, soon began putting people in my life, putting books in my life, putting Bible study opportunities in my life, putting great teaching and mentors and discipleship in my life. It all started with a course I signed up for, taught at a church I didn't even attend, built around developing a "life plan" as a tool for providing focus to a person's spiritual goals.

The mechanism was very simple. One page. The work involved in creating it, of course, was more time-consuming than that, birthed out of much prayer, sharing, and biblical principles. The stated objective was to come from there with a relatively short document that boiled down my unique core priorities to a memorable few, then augmented them with goals, a mission statement, and a practical trajectory for putting all of it into motion.

Hear me on this: I'm not championing any certain method for helping you get honest with yourself and begin putting some things down on paper in terms of where your life needs to be headed. Choose your own path for doing it. The tool is not what's important. But please don't just keep ambling along, doing what is considered normal, assuming everything is cool, caving to your usual comfort areas, all the while letting your family drift along as well. Again, the changes you implement may or may not need to be dramatic swings of difference. Whatever type of analysis you employ to help you sync up a more focused, well-balanced life perspective may lead you to movement by degrees, not by total deconstruction. But a change of some sort is most likely necessary. And God—through prayer, through Scripture, through His Spirit, and through the wise counsel of others—can be counted on to be heavily invested in making sure those changes make a game-changing difference in your family's life and legacy.

In the midst of the process, I discovered a number of attitudes that had become idols in my own heart. Most of them orbited around achievement and accomplishment. As with many people who were raised in church, I grew up infused with a performance-based theology. Not intentionally, I don't think, but that's just how it tended to cash out in my thinking, my self-concept, and how I related with God. I was trained to win and compete. In everything. Results-driven and performance-oriented. The Lord, of course, can sanctify some of that internal drive and use it for His own purposes and ends. But mix it up with the sin in our hearts, as well as the influence of the Enemy, blinding us and taking us off-mission, and we have problems. We end up being dads, like me, perpetuating through our children some of the same lies and faulty spiritual logic that have frustrated us, defeated us, and minimized our view of God, leaving us always striving but never quite satisfied.

So as He began dredging up some of this garbage, helping me see it in all of its starkness and limitation—how it was making me think too small and short-term, even as I tried to think big—He made me want to throw it out and see myself transformed. And in its place (over time) He gave me four words that have come together to show me how transformation is supposed to take place in me: (1) *surrender*, (2) *sacrifice*, (3) *humility*, and (4) *dependence*.

Actually, that's not too bad a group of words for anybody to consider.

Because, Terence, He seemed to be saying, *I can't use you until these four things are present in your life.* Surrender. Sacrifice.

Humility. Dependence. That's where I needed to stay anchored, focused, committed, and growing. It didn't mean my innate tenacity needed to shrink into passivity. I just needed to drive it in a slightly different direction. If I did, I would see my true purpose actually start to make regular appearances in my weekday mornings and afternoons. I'd still be engaged with my passion for business, but its successes would now spill out of greater, more eternally targeted priorities—all through the enabling power of Christ.

And best of all, my family would be the first to experience the blessings.

Paul instructed the Philippians to ground their lives and loves in "knowledge and depth of insight"—and to continue to do it "more and more"—so they would be "able to discern what is best" and would be "pure and blameless for the day of Christ" (Phil. 1:9–10). That's because God's priorities are the *best* priorities. They're the ones that really matter. And they need to be ours too. Otherwise, we can't be everything we were put here to be.

And what's the point if we can't do that?

WHAT'S THE ONE THING?

I don't know what God will choose to do in your heart if you agree to take me up on this challenge, if you determine to call a time-out here and make sure your life is squared up in the direction you truly want to go. Some of the conclusions you'll reach, as He uniquely leads you toward the plans He created you to experience and influence, will be as individual to you as your DNA.

Somewhere in that revelation—assuming you're a parent or,

perhaps, a grandparent or other relative with the responsibility of raising children—will be the mandate of leading and discipling your children in Christ. This is not only your obligation; it is your privilege. A tall order, yes. But what else can truly compare to it?

I recall in those early days as I first began engaging in a real, inquisitive, hungry way with God's plan for my life, He took what I'd been accustomed to doing for so long—writing vision, mission, and value statements for business purposes—and He twisted the kaleidoscope until it lit up with the much fresher colors of my home and my children. So I just started to ask myself these questions and focus on the answers: "What vision do you have for your family? What do you want to achieve with your legacy? If you did nothing else and you died tomorrow, what's the one thing you want to be sure you've accomplished?"

That last one, especially, is a tough question because many candidates are vying for that number one position. Whatever the particular season of your life, many good things would love to hold that ranking, whether we ought to allow them to apply for it or not. But if you had room for only one, what would it be? If God were to show up in the flesh today, at your home or place of business, and ask, "What's the one thing you want Me to do for you so that you can do the one thing you want to do in life?" what would it be?

We need an answer for that. We need to plan for that. The priorities we embrace as a result of it are the vehicles that are going to drive what fills that blank, what lands in that slot. Those priorities are going to reflect our true heartbeat—not who we *think* we are but who we *truly* are. Once we know the person we want to be, God will work through our well-targeted priorities to turn us into that person until that is who we actually become. We all like the sound of that. (Your wife, men, will like the sound of that too.)

And I believe you're ready. Ready to take this bull by the horns. You're starting to realize, as I did, that if you don't know what you want for yourself, for your family, and for your children, somebody else out there does. Hollywood, for example, knows what it wants for your children. The marketers at the dotcoms and the retail dealers know what they want for your children. The school system knows what it wants for your children; perhaps even your children's schoolmates or neighborhood friends know what they want as well.

What about you? Do *you* know what you want for your children?

The *one thing*?

Here's mine. And it all came out of this life plan that God led me to discover and develop. My one thing is "to make Christ known to my kids." That's it. To know Him is to love Him. To love Him is to trust Him. And trusting Him will lead them to a life far beyond what they could ever create for themselves.

If I do nothing else but share the gospel with them (and we'll flesh out what this means as we go along), I'll call it a good life. No regrets. I tell my children all the time, "At the end, if I didn't do anything else right but I shared the gospel with you, I did my job. That's all I really want you to remember me by."

That's why I'm sticking to my life plan. That's why I'm trying to live out my faith, staying consistently under the power and control of the Holy Spirit. I fail at it so often, and I know I'll continue to fail going forward, but—I'm dead serious about this—I go back to the cross every day. *I must*. The cross is all I have. I'm nobody without His mercy and forgiveness. Jesus died to give me grace, and He rose from the grave to give me hope. So I rush back there *every single day* in repentance because I want my kids to see the gospel—to see Christ, not me—to see that His grace is always needed, and yet it's always enough. I want them to see the gospel both shared and lived. I want them to see their dad surrendered, sacrificial, humble, and dependent. I want them to know Christ and what He can do.

That's my plan. And I'm sticking to it.

If we stick together, we all will be able to see it.

CHAPTER 3

STEPS IN THE RIGHT DIRECTION

"To make Christ known to my kids." What if that truly became our one thing? What kind of difference would it make? Not just someday but every day.

Here's why these questions matter so much. I don't think any of us would disagree with the notion that if 100 percent is full capacity on what our personal calendars and career obligations can accommodate, life is always trying to cram about 120 percent, 130 percent, 140 percent—more than 100 percent, anyway—into a space that can hold only so much, no matter how well we multitask or how little sleep we get. So while you and I tend to consider ourselves the exception—that somehow the same rules of capacity don't apply to us, with our clever and capable ways of managing things—guess what? *They do.* So every day, like clockwork, between our varied assortment of have-to-dos and want-to-dos, we each top out by necessity at our maximum 100 percent. And whatever else we intended to include or swap out for something else, all those extra things get stuck off to the side somewhere, undone, untouched, even if we've displaced them with lesser things. That's just the way it is.

And that's why knowing our one thing is so important. When we're clear about what we absolutely *do not want to leave this earth without doing*, we're going to make dead sure not many days pass by when that one thing doesn't factor somehow, to some degree, into our 100 percent. We'll see to it.

But without a plan, we won't.

No matter how much we say we want it.

Dr. Gail Matthews, a psychology professor at Dominican University in San Rafael, California, has conducted research to test for some of the same variables that allegedly went into the classic Harvard Goals Study and Yale Goals Study of the 1950s, both of which have now been debunked as urban legend. Though her current findings aren't quite as dramatic as those numbers from yesteryear appeared to indicate, the facts still remain impressive enough to create some solid conclusions. They confirm that people who don't just *think* about their goals but who (1) write them down, (2) turn them into action points, and then (3) hold themselves regularly accountable for the results are nearly twice as likely to achieve them, by a difference of 76 percent to 43 percent.[1]

That's strong. That will challenge preconceived notions.

Clear, written, actionable plans with built-in accountability work. When we consider the stakes of the plan, in this case, are whether our children will be given deliberate opportunities to own and stretch their Christian faith and experience the real

---

1 Sarah Gardner, "Dominican Research Cited in Forbes Article," Dominican University of California, accessed April 11, 2016, www.dominican.edu/dominicannews /dominican-research-cited-in-forbes-article.

activity of God in their hearts—right here, in our homes, where they can personally see it and feel it—I don't think we have much of a choice to make.

The difference between being halfway successful and almost guaranteed successful is, for us, the difference between lifelong regret and generations-long legacy. It's the difference between *hoping* our kids receive enough spiritual lessons in children's church to navigate a grown-up world, as opposed to *knowing* we've poured Scripture and truth into their hearts at an up-close, personal range, and, as God says in His Word, it "will not return to me empty" (Isa. 55:11). It is worth whatever changes we need to implement in order to make it happen. It is worthy of the same (or greater) level of planning that we would give to *anything* where the success of the matter was significantly important to us.

Looking back, I'd say that's basically where I found myself during that most convicting stage of my life journey as a husband and a parent. I was sure that God was stirring a new fire in me—for Him, for my family. I was sure I needed to do *something* to follow up on it. But what? And how? Hey. It's no humility play on my part to tell you that I did not feel adequate for what I was being led to do. Even these many years later, God and His grace remain the only logical explanations for any fruit that has come from this simple attempt at trusting Him. But that's apparently how He wants it. He loves infusing His Spirit into homes and families whenever parents—especially fathers—say, "You know what? I accept. I know I've failed, and I know I'll keep failing. But if You will show me how, Lord, I will do this. I will follow You in what You've called me to do, and I will lead my family spiritually to the best of my ability."

I believe that's probably where you are. And that's good because it's a large part of the journey. Actually, it's the most essential piece.

But there's something else. And if we really want this for our families, we'll do this part too—because it's a key component in our obedience to this calling, just as much as our eagerness, willingness, and desire for our children to develop as believers are components of the process.

It is this: *we need a plan.*

You may say, "I know. I *want* a plan. But I'm just not really the planning type." Are you sure about that? When you go out looking for the parts and equipment you need for an all-day fix-it project around the house, do you drive aimlessly around town, looking for whatever store might possibly carry what you need? Do you not, instead, have a pretty good idea where to go and what you're hoping to find when you get there—even if your main strategy is to bring the broken piece with you from home and to walk with it up and down the aisles at Lowe's until you find a new one to match?

When vacation time rolls around in the summer, do you gather the kids in the car, bright and early on a beautiful morning, crank the engine, turn around in the driver's seat, and say, "Okay, guys, where does everybody want to go this week? The beach? The mountains? The campground? Your grandparents'? Where?" No. You've already planned your vacation. God has designed us to be planners. He's wired us to do our best work and discover our most reliable path to success when we know what we want and when we know where we're going.

Planning in itself is not the problem. The problem is that we typically spend more time planning our vacations than we spend mapping out a spiritual itinerary for our family. Yet, while we keep making vacation plans, 401(k) plans, exercise plans, and even imaginary plans for what we'd do differently if enough money or opportunity ever came in, too many of us shy away from making the one plan for the one thing that might just do away with our need for making half of those other plans. When we become truly serious about doing something different in regard to the spiritual discipleship of our children, we need to flip the switch to a new kind of planning, and we need to do it now.

WHEN A PLAN COMES TOGETHER

Start somewhere. That's always pretty good advice. And here's another good piece of advice as you try to walk out this particular aspect of His will for your life: use what's currently in your possession—the things God has already given you and shown you how to do well.

That's what God was saying to Moses at the burning bush when He asked, indicating the staff Moses was carrying with him, "What is that in your hand?" (Ex. 4:2). *Let's start with that*, He said. And we know from our knowledge of biblical history, He was able to do quite a bit of work with that basic tool of Moses' trade as a country shepherd.

"What is that in your hand?" In many ways, that's how God directed me to take some first steps in the direction of assuming the spiritual leadership of my family, which led me to a plan I hadn't ever considered. If I hadn't seen this plan work throughout the many years since—in not only my family but also hundreds and hundreds of others—I wouldn't be sitting here today writing a book. I certainly would never dare to pretend I had something worth saying to you. Nothing particularly special about me and my family puts us in a position to speak with any authority on this subject, except that God made us want to take this journey. And then He gave me an idea for how to take a stab at starting it—utilizing a tool that was already close at hand.

During one phase of my career, I'd been introduced to a business solutions strategy known as the Blue Sheet process—a Strategic Selling concept designed by Miller Heiman, a consulting firm that specializes in helping companies enhance sales performance and customer experience. Using this discovery exercise, which examines desired outcomes and objectives based on overall values, culture, environment, and other related components, a company can develop a comprehensive, collaborative, fully operational business plan. The plan doesn't try to push products or services, but, instead, it *actually meets a need* that squares directly with a customer's corporate mission. And, as a further strength of this process, the plan's overall framework or skeleton can be developed in less than an hour usually—or at least in a compact, focused period of time.

I had been through and led this drill numerous times, addressing a wide variety of business applications, and I knew how effective it could be. I wondered, *Could this basic template be laid across a different ideology altogether and still work just as well?* Since I knew I was dealing with some of the same elements—vision, mission, goals, values—was there any reason I couldn't co-opt a proven method like the Blue Sheet process and apply it outside its customary box? To my family and our spiritual growth?

I break down some of this in a little more detail throughout the middle portion of this book, so don't get hung up on any intricacies you may think I'm skipping over right now. The truth is, there *aren't* many intricacies, and there *shouldn't* be. Keeping things simple is important. All I'm trying to communicate right now is that God gave me a plan-development idea based on something I already knew, something that fit how He had made me and had been preparing me, and, I guarantee you, the same will be true for you. He will give you a plan. He will show you the right steps to take.

Bottom line, this is all about trust. It's all about Christ's sufficiency, not ours. You need a plan, yes, but what you and I are trying to do here is so much bigger than just a plan. It's bigger than *you*, it's bigger than *me*, and it will *always* be beyond what we think we can accomplish. God has invested too much in your family not to help you succeed at leading them (as well as yourself) toward becoming true disciples of Christ. And "he who began a good work in you" can be trusted to "carry it on to completion until the day of Christ Jesus" (Phil. 1:6). The sooner you quit worrying about that, the better.

Here's how we got started. We decided to slip out of town for a weekend—just my wife, the kids, and me. We rented a little cabin not too far away from home, where I knew we'd be able to do some of the things we most enjoyed. Mostly compete, like at putt-putt golf. While much of the time was dedicated to nothing other than having fun and hanging out, Wanda and I were determined to allocate a portion of our downtime to sharing a vision with our children that we believed could change our lives forever.

I took a notebook with me that contained my start on a Blue Sheet process for our family's spiritual development. (A sample of our Generational Spiritual Development Plan is in the appendix of this book.) I also brought along a notebook with a Blue Sheet that I'd made for each of the kids. I was fully prepared to be the leader of this operation, but each of us was going to weigh in and see where the Lord was directing us to go.

I don't know how difficult this may or may not sound to you already. Depending on the kind of relationship you and your spouse and your children share, you might be saying, "Uh, Terence, if I tried that, they'd tune me out the minute I opened my mouth." I understand. I'm not blind to some of the challenges that can actively oppose and discourage you. We had some of those too. And still do. But remember, we're not talking about merely implementing a program. We're talking about creating a home and a family environment in which you are learning together, praying together, putting faith into action together, and seeking to unite yourselves together around one rallying point: the gospel of Jesus Christ. And the gospel, by definition, means you will never outgrow your total dependence on God for every opportunity you undertake in seeking your objective. Even as your family's faith begins to grow, even as you get on sort of a roll with it, the pursuit will always involve learning how to stay dependent on and trusting toward Him.

You may as well start out that way, then—by trusting Him— depend on Him to help you and show you how to persevere patiently in what you know to be right.

Thankfully, yes, we were in a mostly good relational space with our kids—ages ten to sixteen at the time. That helps. But in no way is it a deal breaker if you're not. What we have seen from personal experience, both in our own lives as well as in the lives of others, is that when a dad (*especially* a dad) truly accepts the mantle of being the spiritual leader in his home—not just by declaration but by the genuineness of his spirit and desire—the whole flow and foundation of the house suddenly shifts. Dramatically. When it's just the mom trying to hold the family together, praying up a storm in her quiet time and herding everybody off to church every week, she's doing the whole thing against a headwind. The dad is like the invisible elephant in the room. Through his passivity and distractions and conflicting priorities, through his failure to step into his God-ordained role—whether due to fear of failure or lack of interest or whatever—he forces his family to ride through life with the parking brake on. He's a drag on the system, even while he's most likely doing good things and genuinely loving his wife and kids the best he knows how.

But once everybody witnesses the change in him—and they won't be able *not* to notice the change when it stems from the depths of his heart—then start expecting things to thrust into overdrive. They just do. They will. I'm not saying it *can't* happen without a dad fully on board; God wants to do His work in your family regardless. But there is simply something about a father embracing the task of being the spiritual leader in his home that accelerates the whole family into a growth spurt. So don't be surprised, as we were, to see your kids jump all over it.

I remember that weekend well. We sat around after dinner, everybody relaxed and comfortable, while I started to tell the kids about some of the things their mom and I had been talking about and how we thought we might proceed in addressing them. Wanda and I shared our personal Christian testimony, some of which—shockingly—we'd never even talked about before with the children. Not *me*, at least. (And let me just say, you'd be amazed how interesting this is to them, the story of your relationship with Christ. Yet even in devoutly Christian homes, those stories often never get told.) Then we walked them through what we were thinking—how we wanted to begin doing some family devotional sessions but with a plan that would end up making it more than that. We weren't going to let it stop at reading a Bible passage and saying a quick prayer and watching everybody squirm to get back to their rooms, back to whatever they'd been doing when we'd so rudely interrupted them. No, we wanted these family get-togethers to become a springboard, not only for gathering a deeper head knowledge about God and the Bible but also for putting ourselves out there to see what exciting things He might want to do with us as a family—if we really believed Him, if we really put our trust in Him, if we really wanted to discover what our purpose in life was supposed to be.

I didn't have the plan all fleshed out yet. You don't have to either. I don't know how many people back away frustrated from their spiritual responsibilities as parents because they can't seem to come up with a *full curriculum*, something that perfectly fits everybody's ages and attention levels and holds everybody's interest, complete with books and crayons and the whole bit, all buttoned up, top to bottom. The nuts and bolts will come in time. You'll see. But don't lose the significance by getting tangled up in a syllabus. Be willing to start the larger vision and work your way into practice from there. That's the *best* way.

Even if some of your kids are small, let them help craft your family's plan. You want the plan to incorporate some of the things currently on *their* radar, on *their* list of questions and concerns—things you may not even know about until a family conversation begins jarring them loose into the open air. That's the gravy.

That's the good stuff. You don't want your micromanagement to cancel out what everybody truly needs because it's not in line with how you drew it up. Give your kids room to help you. To own it. It's not *your* plan; it's *their* plan. It's God's plan to help everyone grow closer to Christ, to become His active, engaged followers within the various worlds each of you inhabits on a routine basis.

My plan, for example, was for us to try to meet together monthly. "No, Dad," my children declared, "we've got to do it every week." The way my kids were talking in the cabin that Saturday sounded as if they were ready to break out their Bibles and start digging into it, right there, in the next five minutes.

"No, no, I can't do weekly," I said. "Monthly."

Okay, so we settled on biweekly. My first compromise. But that's what I'm talking about. Prepare to make it a shared deal that everybody can buy in to.

Not long after we got back home, a few of my daughter's friends were over at the house. I said, "Hey, I've got a project for you girls this weekend, for all of you. I'll even pay you for it. You can split the money up however you want. But here's the deal: Our family is going to start doing a spiritual growth plan. We've been talking about some of our ideas together, but we're still in the beginning stages of figuring it out." From there, I started to give them the rough-cut description of what we'd been thinking. Then I said, "I want you all to help us draft the first fleshed-out version. I don't want it to be something we cram down our kids' throats. I want to get *your* views on it, as if you were designing it for *your* house and *your* parents. How would you do it? What would you want it to look like?" And they did it.

In our basement one weekend my daughter and a bunch of

her teenage friends helped lay down some of the content that not only became our family's plan to "grow in the grace and knowledge of our Lord and Savior Jesus Christ" (2 Peter 3:18), but—by God's uncanny sense of humor and multiplication—also mushroomed into a workshop course that went global through the outreach of Focus on the Family and has now helped thousands of parents turn their inner hopes for family discipleship into an everyday reality.

Again, only God, right?

I can't do that. And neither can you. Here's where the baby steps of our plans to "make Christ known to our kids" can zoom beyond our oh-so-finite, oh-so-limited capabilities until a once-impossible task turns into the most satisfying sense of mission and accomplishment a man or woman can ever experience.

PART OF A BIGGER PLAN

God had a plan. He's a planner. He planned for Creation, then He spoke all the universe into existence by the power of His Word. He planned for Adam and Eve and the establishment of the human race, then He placed them together in the garden of Eden, where they could enjoy perfect relationship, both with each other and with Him. He even planned for the Fall, knowing exactly what He would do when sin corrupted the earth and all of humankind. As early as Genesis 3, before the story of Scripture was barely two pages old, He was already hinting of His eternal plan to send His Son, Jesus, to "crush" the head of the serpent and provide His people with mercy, forgiveness, protection, and redemption (v. 15). To bring life from death. An incredible plan.

Being God, of course, He could've chosen any way He wanted to communicate this plan to us, to those who would come along in the wake of Adam's depravity, despairing of our sin and needing a Savior. The plan He chose to implement was to inspire the development of a Book—eventually a collection of sixty-six books arranged into almost 1,200 chapters—that would outline in historical, prophetic, poetic, and narrative detail His plan for rescuing His people from the curse of sin, not only to salvage meaning amid our life on earth but also to promise us life forever with Him in glory.

The reason we possess this written plan we call the Bible is not a happy accident of time and good intentions and superior archival preservation techniques. It's the result of an amazing plan by a planning God, who planned before the foundation of the world to deliver His message in written form to generations of His people.

Yet as cosmic and global as these plans of God appear and are, they also are extremely personal, coming right down your street and stopping at your mailbox. For not only did He create families as the core unit of His plan for society, He also created yours. *Your* family. And He has given you, in addition to His written plan, the Holy Spirit of God, to write this plan on your heart.

So I think we can come to a sound conclusion: The reason for all these plans coming together—from Eden through Israel through the worldwide spread of the gospel, down to the very place you call home and the people you share it with—cannot simply be to watch television in separate rooms and prepare everybody's sack lunches in the morning and share birthday cake around the table every now and then. There's too much involved in God's plan to limit it to family photos and pizza nights and the usual hum of the school day and workday. All of those things are part of it, and each contributes to the rub and rhythm of our relationships. But in the midst of all these many things, there's a bigger thing. There is a "one thing." And as the leader of our homes, our responsibility (and again, I say, our privilege) is to make sure the one thing doesn't become consumed by the 120 to 140 percent of things that want to account for everything.

The plan we began in our house many years ago with our family works. Not because we're geniuses or some kind of spiritual giants but simply because we know from God's Word, we know from God's Spirit—we know from our gut—that growing together in our faith is what we're supposed to be doing. And I believe you're as ready as I was to get started.

In the next part of this book, I share with you a seven-step plan designed to take your family into a new experience of growth, unity, and mission. The steps are merely suggestions, but the underlying concept comes with a promise: "Commit your way to the LORD . . . and he will act" (Ps. 37:5 ESV). When God is the One you're trusting to bring about welcome change in your family, you can be sure something special is going to happen. So get ready—to work, yes, but mostly to watch. You're preparing to plant yourself in the center of His will. And that is one exhilarating place for your family to be.

PART II

THE PLAN

CHAPTER 4

FROM DAUNTING
TO DOABLE

L et's talk about what brought you here. You may be at your wits' end with one or more of your kids, and, frankly, you're looking for anything right now that could possibly help fix the trouble and turmoil you're experiencing. Or perhaps you're dissatisfied with the state of your marriage, which has begun to grow increasingly volatile and contentious, or simply more distant and lifeless, until it's starting to affect everybody in the whole house. You're frustrated at how these breakdowns in your relationship as husband and wife are keeping you from being as focused as you should be on what you know your children truly need from you.

On the other hand, your life may be clicking along fine for the most part, but you've started to realize lately, underneath it all, that you're moving too fast, that you're largely being controlled by the chaos. You're passing each other in the hallway, yet you're misreading each other in all the hustle and bustle, just kind of letting the current take you both, not stepping in with a real vision as parents for what God specifically desires for your family.

Whether you've reached this point as a result of several different things, from desperation or determination, or a combination of those things, you're here now. You want this. *And that's great.* I pray the Lord will use some of the upcoming ideas to spur you forward with a fresh dose of confidence.

I'll just say—hopefully, as a little boost of incentive—we've trained parents on these general principles in churches all over the place and in various settings. From what we've been able to measure and monitor in the weeks following those workshops, about 95 percent of the people who go through the process succeed at both completing and implementing their plans. That's just about everybody.

I'm convinced the rationale behind such a high usability rate is not because there's anything so extraordinarily innovative or spectacular about what we're sharing. It's not rocket science. But I do think I can attribute what makes it work to a few distinctives that come into play, whatever your context, in whatever way you try to get things going.

First, the plan is individual to your family. It's not a ten-step prescription, meant to be followed to the letter, like a strict diet or workout plan. The reason those types of programs so rarely pay off the way we envision is because they wrongly assume we all are the same. And they wrongly assume that we're motivated to follow directions, even if in our more zealous, ambitious moments we may perceive the ultimate goal to be worth the grind. To be handed a regimen of orders with which to comply, without any real consideration of what makes our setting and situation unique to us, is like being handed a sentence of failure.

Human beings simply resist conformity to rigid rules and procedures, especially when those rules don't quite seem to apply to us or when we're constantly needing to square-peg this thing to make it match the round holes in our lives.

I'm afraid what actually happens when we adopt somebody else's program for our families is this: we take off one set of handcuffs and put on another. Before, we were shackled by guilt and fear and the paralysis of our own inadequacy and inconsistency. Afterward, however, we're still shackled—this time by legalistic, fill-in-the-blank performance measures that not only fail to reach anyone in the house on a heart level but also incite us all to rebellion, which doesn't exactly make it a blueprint for change or for the cheerful eagerness to keep going.

What's funny, though, is that we still sort of gravitate there. When a task feels too difficult for us—as this one does—we like to be told what to do. I remember in the early days of taking families through this process, we'd present the gist of our plan, hand it out as a written example for people to glean from, and then encourage them to come up with their own individualized plans in response. But what they invariably created for themselves would be a bunch of plans that looked almost exactly like ours and, therefore, looked almost exactly like everybody else's. I'd say, "Wait a minute, guys. Your family and our family are not the same. Our family has *this* kind of background, *we* have kids this age, and we have this particular mix of issues and intangibles. We're not trying to tell you to copy us. We want you to let God lead you toward what fits and what works best for you."

That's what this plan is made to do—to free you from the pressure of checking off other people's boxes as the only way of seeing transformation in your family. Instead, let God use what you already know about your family's makeup, needs, situation, and trajectory to construct a plan all your own because, after all, we're not racing one another. We're not prepping to meet some kind of standardized religious requirements. Nor are we putting ourselves in the running for Christian family of the year. We're just helping our kids love the Lord and live the kind of joyful, purposeful lives that flow from that. And the best way to do this is to build a plan that's yours and yours alone from the start.

Second, the plan has no age limits or time limits. Perhaps the biggest challenge that hinders any kind of family discipleship plan is its inability to accommodate wide ranges of age and maturity. Let's say, for example, you have a five-year-old, an eight-year-old, and a twelve-year-old—maybe one even younger, one or two even older. Somehow you're supposed to sit everyone down, open up the Bible, and deal with it in a way that doesn't sail right over your little ones' heads or bore your teenagers half to death.

Yes, that's a problem. It is always the case with plans that are built by somebody else for your family to squeeze into. They never come off just right. They feel fake. Awkward. Forced. Incomplete. But when, instead, you're constructing your own plan, based on an intimate knowledge of your family that no one else can decipher as well as you, each child is then able to grow toward certain goals that fit the stage of life he or she currently occupy. (We'll talk more specifically about this when we get to chapter 9. You're going to like that part.)

But beyond the pressure of conforming to somebody else's standards—and beyond the pressure of keeping everyone in the family entertained—this plan also helps you shake free from the pressure of needing to *finish*, to cover a certain amount of material in a certain amount of time.

People routinely tell us, "I wish we would've started this sooner." I know. You and me both. It's the same thing we've often said as well. The Devil wants not only to keep you discouraged by this nagging gravel of regret but also to shortchange the effectiveness of what God is accomplishing in your family by pressuring you to hurry up and move through the program, to stick to an artificial schedule or be discouraged because you're running behind. But leading your family spiritually is less about compiling an impressive list of subjects you've covered and more about giving God whatever amount of time He desires for His truth to be absorbed throughout your whole system. The goal is not to get through a set amount of coursework but to become more like Christ.

I shared earlier how our family continues to do biweekly devotionals together by telephone even though all our kids are now grown and out of the house. Again, this may or may not work for you the way it does for us. And even for us it may or may not always stay this way forever and ever. Probably won't. That's okay. Even though we didn't get started in earnest until our kids were ten and up, we've still enjoyed nearly twenty years of quality time getting to know Him, getting to know one another, and experiencing His plans for us as individuals and as a family. And we're *still* not finished. But we're sure a long way from where we started. And that's what is important. Built on that model, our kids (like yours) can carry this plan forward into their own homes and marriages and families—changing it, modifying it, mixing it up—as God keeps streaming it out across the generations, even after my wife and I are dead and gone. So it *never* needs to finish. There's simply no rush—just the rush of watching Him excite and encourage your children as His Word takes hold of them.

And third, the plan holds you accountable to your family. As we've already seen verified by both research and experience, accountability is an imperative for any plan that we're committed to doing well and maintaining long-term, no matter what the field or purpose of it. So I suppose, looking at it that way, the process of family discipleship and generational legacy I'm going to show you is no more compatible to accountability than any other kind of plan.

But then again, maybe it is more so. Since it's designed to be crafted and customized with the help of each member of the family, this means your spouse and kids represent an ongoing, built-in accountability force all by themselves. They'll be expecting you to stick to this—and they'll be the first to notice and comment on it if you're not. And if you choose to add the extra layer of an outside prayer partner or Bible study group—one that helps you answer and keep tabs on your commitments—you're then doubly insured against drifting away from your promises to your family. But however you approach it, accountability will help make your devotion, loyalty, and enthusiasm for the entire process stronger and sturdier.

I'll tell you how we always infuse a tier of accountability into the seminars we lead. When the session is over—now, prepare to be blown away by the sophistication of this method—we instruct everyone to tear out a piece of paper, write their phone number on it, wad it up into a tight ball, and then toss it across the room. Fastball, curveball, gentle lob, or low liner, doesn't matter. Whoever's paper wad you catch or pick up off the floor, that's your accountability partner.

The responsibilities entailed in this job description are actually very simple. Fifteen days after the event, you're to call the number on that crumpled-up piece of paper you brought home and ask the person on the other end of the phone one simple question: "Have you started your plan yet?" That's it. The only acceptable answer to this question—the only answer you're looking for—is yes or no. Not, "Well, I've been busy." Not, "You know, I've been meaning to get around to it." None of that.

Just *yes*. ("Good. Way to go!")

Or *no*. ("Come on then! Get started.")

Then hang up.

You'd be surprised, when at the next accountability marker, fifteen days after that—thirty days total, when they come back to church for a follow-up session—how that single little telephone bump prompted noticeable action. As I said, it's about 95 percent effective. And in one way or the other, I'm sure you'll find the gentle pressure of accountability helpful in your own situation as well.

Accountability along with age-stage *flexibility* and individual *personality* are the three biggest reasons why I can commend the basic premise of this plan to you. In God's hands, it can do what you want it to do in your children's lives.

Fact is, it can do much more.

GOOD GOES AROUND

I recall a husband and wife who came to us once. They didn't have a clue about what it meant to develop a spiritual plan for their family but realized—with two young kids, each right below school age—they needed to do something more than what they were doing, which, basically, was not doing anything.

As is the case with many parents in that active, high-energy phase of life, their marriage had been slowly taking a backseat to the exhausting, child-centered challenges of each day's little dramas. They never really sat down and discussed their marriage much, except in short-tempered bursts of frustration and rarely in constructive ways that led to any consensus solutions. They each knew their marriage was becoming less enjoyable and less connected than either of them wanted it to be. And as far as their parenting? Well, they felt as though they were probably doing that part okay. Or were they? They couldn't really tell.

They did stuff together, went to church together, and took trips to the zoo and the aquarium together—all the things you do with excitable little kids around the house. But just because they'd gotten pretty good at overseeing noise and movement, did that mean they were fulfilling their main functions as parents? Not sure. And they wanted to start being sure. After all, school was coming soon. Things were going to be changing. They'd have less direct influence on their children. More worries. More issues. Maybe trying to get a better spiritual handle on things would keep those worries and issues to a minimum. They thought being more deliberate and systematic in training their children spiritually would make them better parents. More focused. More on top of things. While they soon began to see a few little encouraging improvements here and there, enough to make them glad they'd chosen to zero in on the developing faith of their growing children, something else also started happening. Something they didn't expect.

Their marriage began to improve markedly too.

They could tell they were drawing closer again as a couple.

When you think about it, why *shouldn't* this happen? Whenever a leader starts bringing clearer direction, focus, and goals to an organization, you expect to see a turnaround over time in bottom-line sales growth or market share—in whatever way the organization measures itself. But those aren't the only places you generally start to see welcome change. You also see it in better productivity, employee satisfaction, team spirit, creative thinking. These all start pointing up, becoming more positive. The same thing happens at home. The leader steps in with clearer direction, focus, and goals for the family, and pretty soon little pockets of improvement start popping up all over the house, in everyone's relationships, in places that initially weren't at the center of attention.

One of the things that sparks these changes, of course, is prayer. Most families today spend little to no time together in prayer, beyond maybe a mealtime blessing or the kids' bedtime prayers. But what do you think happens when now you're holding hands and praying on purpose, at the drop of a hat, as standard operating procedure for how your household functions? A little more unity begins to build between everyone.

Plus, you're simply talking more, about more significant things, not every second of the day but more often than you once did. The practice of simply being intentional about asking your kids what they learned at church, what they see in a Bible story, or what they want you to be praying about causes new kinds of conversations to happen. You're worshiping differently. You're scheduling your day differently. You're noticing things more. You're doing little kindnesses that used to fly through your head on occasion but rarely made it all the way down to the ground, into action. Maybe you're even eating *together* again, whereas, until now, you had gotten into the habit of grabbing a plate and going off in all directions.

The point is, life beforehand had been scattered throughout each person's own little world, a spinning network of loosely connected planets that basically functioned independently of one another. But now you've brought the center of gravity into one place—the spiritual direction of your family. And now, as a group, you more consistently orbit around the plans and the will and the Word of God, which is starting to affect not only your children but also you and your marriage. And probably more than that.

That's what you can legitimately expect as God begins to work through your courageous sense of humility and willingness, creating a plan to lead your family on the most important journey of your lives. Of *all* of your lives.

JUST DO IT

I said at the outset of this chapter what I know to be true: many people arrive here out of desperation, looking for a way to fix what has gone wrong with their families. I wouldn't call this plan of ours a "fix"—as in a "quick fix." Life doesn't typically operate in terms of quick fixes, and we shouldn't keep jumping from one bandwagon to the next in search of one. But what people really mean when they say this—and they've said it to me quite often through the years—is that if they could just change the way their kids behave, everything would be okay. "Can your plan help us do that, Terence?"

I'm all for changing behavior—starting with my own. And

I believe the Holy Spirit is not only *capable* of changing our behavior, but He is, in fact, the *only* way behavioral changes are made in *any* of us. Therein lies the secret of not only what makes this plan successful but also what shows us where God wants our minds and hearts to be as we undertake this daunting yet doable process.

I go back to those four words: (1) *surrender*, (2) *sacrifice*, (3) *humility*, and (4) *dependence*. Only God knows what He will choose to do in your children's lives as you begin actively leading them toward the gospel, toward the Scripture, into prayer, and into worship. But even I know where it's likely to lead *you*—the same place it's led me—to many different moments in life when you see more clearly the gulf between your righteousness and His, where you see His saving love for you expressed through Christ's sacrifice on the cross, and where you see the power of the Holy Spirit as your only source of equipment for living out this new kind of life—and its new behavior—that's now available to you.

That's usually where the "fix" needs to happen first. In you. In me. In our *hearts*. In *all* of our hearts, not just in our *behavior*.

So I want to encourage you. You're doing a great thing here. You're doing what God has called you to do. The way forward, of course, may end up becoming a little more hilly and curvy than you'd prefer. It often does. But even if you get turned sideways or turned around, you're always going in the right direction when you're seeking His will for your life and family.

I can remember the exact spot in the road where the Lord showed me that we'd done the right thing, that He was obviously driving the train. My son was away at college in Nashville at the time and had been gone from home for a couple of years.

We were scheduled to do one of our Sunday night phone calls as a family, nine o'clock eastern standard time, every other week, as always. As we were wrapping up that night, a little after ten, my son told everyone good-bye, said he was in the middle of rehearsing a stage show he was producing at school and people were waiting on him.

"You mean they're waiting on you right now?" I asked.

"Yeah."

Forgive me the little pause of disbelief I had at this point. I sort of laughed and said, "Uh, production costs money, doesn't it, son? You mean you broke off from the show you were in charge of? To come do this phone call with us?"

"Yeah," he said. "I just told them I needed to go, that I had something to do between nine and ten."

"Like what?" the other kids had asked him.

"I told them my family does this phone call on Sunday nights for an hour."

I was floored. Here was our quiet, subdued, twentysomething son, off at college, choosing to worship and pray and talk over the Word with his family, even if it meant letting the lights go dark on his rehearsal for a solid hour with people standing around waiting for him on the last night of their weekend.

I knew it was real then. That's when I knew what the Lord was truly capable of doing. If He could take a guy with all my faults and shortcomings, with my little bit of Bible knowledge and background, and create a plan that could work well enough to make a busy college kid not want to blow off doing devotions with his mom, his sisters, and me, at the risk of severely inconveniencing his schedule, then this God of ours could do anything. With me.

And with you.

So wherever you feel inadequate, unprepared, woefully imperfect, and totally overwhelmed, realize you're in the ideal place where He can do some of His greatest work, revealing His awesome strength through your aw-shucks weaknesses. The transformation He wants to bring about in you, your marriage, your children, your family—and yes, in the generations to come—in your *legacy*—is not dependent on what you think you cannot do. It's only dependent on the One who truly cannot fail. And that makes your job as doable as it can get.

CHAPTER 5

UP AND DOWN THE FAMILY TREE

Step 1: Discover Your Spiritual Heritage

I have an aunt who *loves* genealogy. She's the kind of relative who shows up at family reunions with all the collated handouts to distribute or with full albums of old photographs to lay across the picnic tables, tagged by specific names and dates. Imagine her delight when, as part of her digging around for bits and shreds of family historical information, she came across a well-worn Bible that appeared to have been used by one of our ancestors as far back as the mid-1820s.

Turns out this Bible belonged to my great-great-great-grandmother. And within its pages, this matriarch of our family had written out by hand the names of her children and other family members for whom she was specifically praying.

Based on records like these (as well as others), my aunt has deduced that during the early to middle part of the 1800s, many of the women in my direct family tree were women of faith. The men? Not so much. Interestingly (or consequently?), most of these forefathers of mine during this period were dying off at early ages—thirties, forties—younger than average.

But the records seem to indicate a shift occurring in my family line after my great-great-grandfather came to Christ. From that point on, the men began to live longer. And while this fact alone is certainly not enough to prove direct correlation, a clear thread does start to emerge from the written history, indicating the presence of a renewed spiritual interest in their lives, as well as evidence of active leadership in their churches and their homes as husbands and fathers.

I actually knew my great-grandmother, whose husband (my great-grandfather) was a man of faith. I knew my grandfather as well and, of course, my own father. And I knew them all to be men who were serious about their work, serious about their education, serious about the church, and serious about God. Therefore, while the spiritual legacy of my family appears to go back almost two hundred years, I know for sure it goes back four generations because I have the memories or the documentation to back it up.

This makes my children at least a sixth generation of believers in my family. Think of it. *Six* generations. That's more than a hundred years of spiritual impact.

So when my *great-great-grandfather* was praying for his family, he was also praying for me and for mine. When my *great-grandfather* was worshiping and thanking God for the blessings he'd been given in his life, he was handing down praise as an inheritance to all of us who would follow in his generational footsteps. When my *grandfather*, a deacon in his church, welcomed us to his home for Sunday dinner every week, the words of wisdom that flowed into my life from those afternoon conversations were flowing right through me, eventually flowing down to my children. And when my *father* was setting an example of Christian integrity and work ethic in our home, he wasn't only inspiring those of us who grew up around him and learned from his influence. He was investing also in his grandchildren—my children—and those who will one day follow after them.

That's part of the message I wanted to share with my kids during that first little weekend retreat, where we started to talk about launching a new spiritual plan for our family. I told them this journey that we were starting was hardly the beginning. They were already swimming in an ocean of legacy that had been streaming in their direction for a hundred years or longer.

I love the thought of that. The *reality* of that. Think of the kind of perspective this truth can plant in a child's mind and heart. Kids—even more so than adults—bookend their daily lives inside a fairly confined frame of reference. Except for the times when they're wishing Christmas would hurry up and come or dreaming of becoming a pro football player, they generally concentrate on today or what's coming up tomorrow. It's usually not a wide field of vision. But I wanted my kids to see themselves as part of something much bigger than that. A *hundred times* bigger than that. I wanted to show them how their God, who'd actually been grooming their lives for eternity, had also graciously placed them on earth within a direct, hundred-year continuum of spiritual blessing. Not only that, but I wanted them to receive this legacy with the sense of gratitude it deserved, realizing that not every family has this kind of Christian heritage as a reference point.

That's what a look at family history can do.

AMAZING DISCOVERIES

I remember a woman running up to me after the part in our workshop where I talk about this subject and looking as if an enormous light bulb had just flashed above her head. She apparently was the "aunt" in her family who'd made genealogy one of her fun little hobbies and interests. And this slight adjustment of focus I'd introduced opened up a whole new world of possibilities for her. "I'd always just done this genealogy stuff to gather information," she said, "you know, to link this person to that person. I'd only seen it as a research exercise. I'd never even *thought* about approaching it from a *spiritual* standpoint, as a way of helping us carry on our parents' and grandparents' legacy of faith."

Right. She got it. This is not just meant to be a history lesson, a book report. It's much richer, much deeper than that. The spiritual history of your family helps you draw your little circle of household existence inside a much larger, much more purposeful ring of influence, one that rolls backward as well as forward.

And that's why, although this overall plan for family discipleship I'm presenting to you doesn't come with requisites, I believe you'll find this particular one an exceptional way to get started.

Nobody ever drew out anything like this for me when I was growing up. Then again, they didn't really *need* to. My grandfather and grandmother, for instance, actually lived with us for a short period of time, as did my great-grandmother later on. And even when close family members like these weren't physically living in our house, they were typically only a few streets away in the same neighborhood or a short distance across town. So the reason I inherently knew a lot about the individual members of my extended family was because we saw one another all the time.

I remember, for example, playing many losing games of checkers with my grandfather. ("Anytime you want to win one," he'd say, "just let me know.") I can still remember standing around talking with him while he worked on the car or the lawn mower—or anything else of his or anybody else's, it seemed, that needed fixing. I remember eating homemade biscuits at the breakfast table with my other grandfather as we talked about life and the Lord and whatever else might come up in casual conversation over cups of his favorite tea.

I knew these people. I knew their stories.

But those days, for the most part, have come and gone. Families who settle down in one place, especially the same place where their moms or dads grew up, and then stay there for the rest of their lives, are the exceptions to the modern rule. In our case, for instance, we moved our kids nine times in eleven years. And by the time we finally put down some semipermanent roots, we were a long drive away from either place where Wanda and I were born and raised. So while our children were familiar with some of their relatives and had visited them from time to time, these people weren't a regular part of our kids' experience. They were virtually strangers to one another even though they shared a heredity of blood and common ancestry. Good chance your kids are in the same boat, I'd imagine, in one way or another.

And I tell you, our kids *ate this ancestry search up.* They wanted to know more. They wanted to know stuff that I didn't know either, which set us off on a search together to see what else we could find.

But the main objective, again, outside of piquing healthy curiosity, is identifying the spiritual roots and branches in your family tree. It's a snapshot of where your family has been, what God has done, and how you and your children fit into that picture—the *spiritual* picture, not just the blanks on a genealogical chart. It's a way for each of you (especially your kids) to develop a new sense of belonging, a deeper sense of gratitude, a broadening sense of time and identity. It's a new reason for keeping up the momentum begun by people who lived in earlier days but whose lives still have a bearing on what God is doing in *your* lives, in *your* day.

All right, I can see your mind is already working, so let's break here for a couple of questions. Here are a few I've heard consistently: "What if there's not much, if any, Christian heritage on my family tree? What if, as far as I know, I'm a first-generation believer?"

No problem. In some ways your situation offers you a little more pioneering excitement than those of us who grew up being taken to church and taught about the Lord for as long as we can remember.

It starts with *you* now. You're the first in what, by God's grace, could represent a completely new fork in the direction of your family legacy. I realize, of course, you can't *make* your children become Christians. Salvation is not an inheritable commodity. You can plant the seeds and water them well; only God can give life and growth. But you stand now at the threshold of an incredible opportunity that's as rich with spiritual potential as your past has perhaps been bereft of it. Not only have you been given the privilege of impacting future decades and centuries with the witness of Christ's forgiving love, but you can also go back now into the buried root system of your family tree and patiently seek opportunities both to share and exemplify gospel truth with generations past as God opens those doors.

You're on the leading edge of what could become a fountain-head of Christian influence flowing through your kids' lives and into the future, hopefully, for hundreds of years, if the Lord waits that long to return. Isn't that cool to think about? Perhaps you missed a lot by not knowing Christ from a younger age, by not being surrounded with people all along who could help you grow in your faith so you wouldn't have to learn it all so quickly as a grown-up. But now, because of your eagerness to impart biblical grounding for your own children's lives, you can help ensure that another generation will not grow up without know-ing, without being able to remember who God is and what He can do—because your children will see it and know it for themselves. That's pretty exciting.

"Well, our family does have some Christians in it, but it also has a lot of trouble and brokenness and breakdown—some of which our kids know about, some they don't. It's not a very pretty picture, really. Not much of a spiritual legacy."

Here's where each of us can benefit from a paradigm shift: the same adjustment that helps us view our genealogy from a spiritual rather than a biological perspective needs to come all the way down into our hearts, where we can view the entirety of life from a spiritual vantage point as opposed to a physical one. This is not how we're wired, of course. It's not our default. But it's the basis for truly understanding the gospel and truly under-standing ourselves.

If given our way, we'd like to be known for how wonderful we are, how successful we are, how strong we are, how wise we are.

Only one problem: we're *not* wonderful. "Wonderfully *made*," yes, by a wonderful God (Ps. 139:14), but not so wonderful in the execution; none of us are (Rom. 3:10–18). That's what led Paul the apostle to say, both of himself and of us, "If I must boast, I will boast of the things that show my weakness. . . . so that Christ's power may rest on me. . . . For when I am weak, then I am strong" (2 Cor. 11:30; 12:9–10). Our glory is not found in what we do and accomplish but found in what God can do and accomplish with such imperfect, uncooperative, intractable, unmanageable pieces of building material.

Like us.

And like our families.

If life wasn't real, if we could spin the story any way we wanted, we'd strike some things from the record that don't cast us and our family in the most favorable light. There wouldn't be any divorces. Wouldn't be any alcoholism. Wouldn't be any unwed pregnancies. Wouldn't be *anything* that required footnoting or justifying or further explanation. But reality begs to differ. The good mingles with the bad. And while even our good is ultimately indebted to God's favor and blessing and the kindness of His mercy, so also the bad—both in ourselves and in our families—is living proof that He continues to seek us, that He continues to persevere with us, that His Word and His faithfulness will not be outmuscled or outmatched by whatever kind of sinful rebellion tries to stand in His way.

In God's economy there are no leading families in society. No haves and have-nots. There's just *your* family. And *my* family. With lots of baggage and brokenness, even in the "best of families." But everything that turns up from digging into our family's spiritual past is intended—good or bad—to point ultimately toward God's plan and how He's kept working with us. And this same God, with His same plan, intends to keep working now through your nuclear family—through both the good and the bad—to bring to Himself the glory due His name.

And that's pretty exciting too.

CARRY IT FORWARD

"I will open my mouth with a parable," one of the psalm writers said. "I will utter hidden things, things from of old—things we have heard and known, things our ancestors have told us. We will not hide them from their descendants; we will tell the next generation" (Ps. 78:2–4).

I want to lay down a challenge for you here—a challenge not to "hide" these things from "their" children. *Their* children? You mean *our* children? Yes. And no. As much as they're *your* children, they're also the children of your ancestors—your parents and grandparents. And they need to know these people's stories, even as your children have come to know yours.

Some of the greatest treasures at the Chatmon household are recordings from in-person interviews we conducted with a number of men and women in our family's past. We don't have interviews, of course, from those who died before we started the recordings. And those whom we do have on tape will each pass away in due course. As will I. As will you. But we must not let their stories die. We must not "hide them from their children" (NKJV). We must make these memories available to be seen and heard, not only for "the next generation," but for many next generations to come—so that they, unlike us, can experience for themselves the great-great-greats in their family line whose faith forms a years-long connection throughout the decades and centuries.

In chapter 7, we'll be looking at your family's vision and how to encapsulate it into a vision statement that you can keep in front of one another as a rallying point for how you think and operate. In our family, as we sought to identify what we wanted our vision to be, we landed on one that we've also shortened into a simple motto: "Unity in the Spirit." That's our aim. That's what we want to increasingly embody throughout our lives together. And one of the activities that feeds into this deep desire is the personal awareness of our spiritual unity, not only with one another and with our contemporary brothers and sisters in Christ but also with those from our family's past with whom we share believing faith.

Your family's vision, of course, may be something else entirely as you think through what makes you distinctive and unique. But all of our families can benefit and be enriched by learning the stories of our predecessors, captured, if possible, for all posterity.

It's a little quirky how the things people find so common-place, if given enough years and generational distance, become valuable collectors' items. A letter opener or a sewing basket that once was merely something that sat around on our grandparents' desk or beside one of their favorite chairs is now an heirloom, a treasure, something we're so glad didn't get thrown away when they downsized their homes or graduated to their eternal one.

The same is true of their stories. They may not seem so unusual or extraordinary. Not to them. They may not have even thought about some of these stories in "my goodness, I can't *remember* when." But these stories are precious and fleeting. They belong to the legacy that God has chosen to create within your family.

I encourage you to give some thought to this task if you haven't already. Interview your family members, particularly the older ones. Ask them questions. Find out how they came to Christ. Find out who was inspirational to them in keeping their faith alive and burning. Find out some of the hardships and struggles that put them to the harshest of tests and how God led them through the storms with greater trust and dependence on His loving faithfulness. Find out what they remember about their own parents and grandparents, about their siblings and other relatives. Find out what they recall affected them when they were the current age of your children or what they remember thinking about or wanting to become when they were that age.

I realize, thanks to our technological advances, we now have unprecedented access to websites and databases that can churn up previously unknown material from our family's past. But think of the amount of unknown material that exists only in the temporary hard drive of your family elders' memory banks. And answer this: What else were you planning to do next Saturday that would be more important to your legacy than spending an afternoon with the camera rolling at your parents' or grandparents' or aunt's or uncle's house?

These are the people who go back with you further than anybody else in your life. Yet I'll bet there are many priceless gems of experience from their personal histories that you've never heard, and certainly your kids have never heard. As James wrote, "You do not have because you do not ask" (James 4:2). Just think what you could "have" if you did.

You've probably talked enough with these loved ones of

yours about the weather in their area, the status of their arthritis, and other such smatterings of small talk that spill out when you catch up by phone or whatever. But you and your children could move the decimal point several placeholders on your overall blessing quotient by seeking *real life* with these people. Whether some of them are talkative or soft-spoken, you need what these various characters in your family can reveal about what they've learned, what they've seen, what they've experienced, and what they know. Prepare for some unforgettable moments to come to life as you jog their memories.

A CHARGE TO KEEP

Abraham understood it. "For I have chosen him," God said, "so that he will direct his children and his household after him to keep the way of the LORD" (Gen. 18:19).

Moses understood it. "The LORD, the God of your fathers—the God of Abraham, the God of Isaac and the God of Jacob . . . is my name forever, the name you shall call me from generation to generation" (Ex. 3:15).

Seems wise, then, that we and our children should understand it—that God doesn't operate merely within seventy- or eighty-year life spans, none of which is any more than a tiny blip on the radar screen of eternity. Something great happens when we realize we're playing in a much bigger pool than we thought and that His plans for us can actually outlive us by measures of centuries.

You probably came to this book and this idea the same way I came to it, asking God to help you lead your family to love His

Word and do His will. What I hope becomes clear, if nothing else, from the upshot of this chapter is that the effects of this noble desire of yours can actually carry on beyond your immediate intentions. The value of taking up this weighty responsibility is a promise you're making to people you don't yet know—some you'll never know until eternity.

When the Lord instructed Moses to ordain Aaron and his sons as the first generation of priests over Israel, Moses led them through a number of ceremonial reminders to help them grasp the significance of their new office. The role they were initiating under God's direction would first be carried out among the people who made up the nation of Israel at that time in history. But the role of the priesthood would actually be carried forth across many other generations to follow, beginning with these ordinary men who'd been commissioned to a role of important spiritual leadership. So I note with interest how, at the culmination of their initial training period, they were commanded to remain at the tabernacle day and night for a full week and to "keep the LORD's charge" (Lev. 8:35 HCSB), to follow what God had commanded them, to pay special heed to what He'd taught them.

Keep the Lord's charge. That's how I'd describe what four generations of ordinary people in my family did and have done for me, out of devotion to the Lord. They stood at their post. They held their position. They did what they'd been instructed to do by the Word, and they delivered a heritage of faith right down into the delivery room where I was born.

Today I want to link arms with these saints to "keep the Lord's charge" for my family, knowing that just as their faithfulness extended beyond them to a *sixth* generation—represented now by Wanda's and my children—my own faithfulness can now be part of delivering a legacy of faith to another hundred years of children down the line.

Come join me in this humble endeavor. When you're fighting off another temptation toward sin tomorrow, realize you're fighting not only for your own purity but also for the benefit of your children, and maybe others yet to be born who will grow up in the wake of a godly family line. When you're feeling too tired or busy to pray this evening, realize you're interceding to the One who's already laying plans for the spiritual fruit to be harvested in generations ahead of you. When you're not sure you can make the sacrifices entailed in leading your family to love and cherish their relationship with Christ, realize you're making an investment whose earning potential can't even be measured in currency values.

I don't want to stop at a hundred years. I want to keep it going. We've been given too much, whether in legacy or potential, even to think about backing away from this now. Step out into the ocean that connects you by God's divine action with those who've gone before, as well as with those who are still to come. It's the perfect position for making a hundred years' or more worth of difference.

CHAPTER 6

THE STORY OF YOUR LIFE

Step 2: Articulate Your Testimony

I f you've been around church for any amount of time, I'm sure you've heard quite a few Christian testimonies and other presentations of the gospel: maybe from a guest speaker sharing his life story as part of the worship service or during the get-acquainted session in a new-members' Bible study class. Maybe you've attended an FCA banquet or a weekend conference with a group from church and listened intently. Hopefully, not a day or week goes by when you're not brought face-to-face at some point with the beautiful, undeserved mercy of the gospel, whether from the pulpit or the Communion table or any number of different places.

Those are inspiring moments. In fact, if you are in the habit of asking people how they first came to faith in Christ, many of them probably will tell you it happened during a church service or some special event. Many teenagers, for instance, receive Christ at youth camp. As adults they still can remember how a summer pastor or a dorm counselor brought the gospel right down to where they could hear it and understand it. Others may point back to their college days, to their experiences with a campus ministry, when they were truly drawn to the Lord for the first time, even if they grew up around Christianity and thought they knew what it was all about. Others could tell a much more dramatic story of how their lives hit the skids and totally bottomed out, how they showed up in tears one night on an old friend's doorstep, begging for somebody to pray for him or her. And all of that is great. Thank God for it. Let's keep doing it. More and more of it.

But, you know, while I realize it may not create the same amount of zing and emotional flair, I have a feeling there's probably no match for the kind of testimony that simply says, "How did I become a Christian? Through my parents. I'd say that's where I learned the gospel—through what my parents lived out at home, what they showed me, what they shared with me."

Show me a child who can truthfully and unashamedly say something like that, and I can show you not only a person who's likely been (or will likely be) spared some of life's most regrettable wastes of time but also a young man or woman who probably is committed to living faithfully for Christ for the long haul. I'm not making absolute promises here, of course. I'm just speaking in likelihoods and generalities: if given the choice, you and I would take that kind of testimony from our kids above any other story they could possibly tell.

That's why I'm of the firm conclusion that the most important story *you* can tell is the story of how Christ specifically and uniquely made Himself real to you.

As I said before—and I'm sad to say it, although I couldn't help but say the same thing of myself, too, for many years—if you're in the vast majority of believing parents, your personal testimony is a story your kids have probably never heard. Not in its entirety, at least. Maybe in tiny bits and pieces. Offhand. Here and there, when it happened to come up, but not on purpose. And not when you had their full attention while you were sharing it.

For me, for my wife, it was that weekend at the lake with our kids. That was the first time we'd deliberately talked with them in much detail about three important phases of time: (1) our lives *before* Christ, (2) how we *came* to Christ, and (3) our lives *after receiving* Christ. Pretty simple, really. That's the basic outline of a person's Christian testimony. But inside this fairly generic template is the story that not only reveals God's generational work amid that spiritual family history of yours (like we talked about in the last chapter). It also reveals the one-of-a-kind fashion in which His Spirit personally found *you* in your sins and transformed you amazingly from very much dead to very much alive. I don't care how nice and neat and well-mannered you were when you were younger. I don't care if all you've ever known was church, church things, and church people, or if you've never doubted God's love for you, not for a minute. The Bible says your story (which is actually *His* story) is a resurrection story. That makes it pretty spectacular, no matter how it all came together.

Your kids deserve to know that story. I'd even say they'll be fascinated by that story, whether they let on immediately or not. And I can promise you they'll never forget it. It's the most important story you'll ever tell them.

- How you lived before you met Christ
- The events that led to your meeting Christ
- How your life has changed since meeting Christ

No one knows that story better than you do. And who else needs to hear it more than your own kids? From your own mouth?

FROM PERSONAL EXPERIENCE

I keep thinking, while I'm writing this, how frightened and hamstrung we tend to feel, believing we're simply not capable of leading our families spiritually. We worry we don't know enough, haven't studied enough, can't be authoritative enough, won't be able to answer their questions well enough. But listen, your kids don't need you to be the answer man (or woman), some kind of walking Bible concordance or encyclopedia who sees all, knows all, tells all. All they need to see from you is a *changed* man, a *changed* woman—somebody who's walking the best he or she can, yielding to the lordship of the Holy Spirit, and imperfectly falling forward into Christ's arms every single day.

That's why the best way to get started on this journey is by opening up with material you already know by heart or can fairly easily find out: (1) your family history and (2) your personal story. Commentaries and Bible studies and day-by-day walking with the Lord will naturally always be there for you as you move forward, helping you learn and grow and build upon the solid foundation of what His Word can teach you as a person and as a family. But the best place to start is where you are now. Start with where you've been. Start with what's already going on. Start with what's specifically yours, just the way you've experienced it.

Your story.

God's story.

Don't ever discount the value of that story.

Yet even here, I'm afraid, we can often lose ourselves in needless complication and worry. Such as, "What if my testimony isn't exciting or powerful enough?" Friend, it's the story of how God sought you by His grace, saved you from your sins, brought you into His family, and promised you an eternity with Him in paradise. What's not amazing about that? If we were somehow able to give a person a gift of that magnitude, the greatest joy in our lives would be hearing them tell other people about it, wouldn't it?

"Well, how much should I share? Maybe I don't really want my kids to know some of the things I did in my past." Yes, and you know what? I'd probably tend to agree with you. So feel the freedom to make a personal call on that part. You're the one who knows best what seems appropriate to your children and their ages, just as you're the one who's most aware of those details that probably deserve another time or place for discussion—or maybe *never* need a time and place, depending on whether the opportunity ever seems necessary or helpful. The only important thing to tell your kids is this: you're a sinner, and the Lord Jesus Christ is the Redeemer. And if you'll just be as transparent as you feel He's calling you to be, I'm sure His grace will still be the hero of your story, no matter how far into specifics you decide to go.

The only way you can mess this up is by not telling them your story at all, by assuming they already know your testimony and already know what Jesus can do to save.

But here's something you can assume they *do* know: they know whether you mean what you're saying or not. And here's where I want to jump in and offer the kind of encouragement that every one of us needs to hear from time to time. If that third part of your testimony—the part about how Christ even now is continuing to change your life—is something you're not feeling too good about, about how you've been living lately, there's a good way to deal with that.

The first thing is to just admit it. It's okay. None of us, frankly, have really been all that happy with how we've maximized the potential that God's grace has made available to us. Maybe *some* people. Maybe. But if so, I'd probably question how honest they're being with themselves, or whether they've kind of gotten a little mixed up on who deserves the real credit for making something good come out of someone like them, out of *anyone* like us. So now's the time to quit worrying about the past. I'm serious. It's okay.

But the day you tell this story to your kids would probably be a good day to tell them they can expect to see some changes because your testimony isn't over. It's still going on. It's still being written. The Lord has much more work He wants to do in you and in me. And as you and I keep drilling down deeper into Christ and His Word—as we ask Him to help us live with true surrender, sacrifice, humility, and dependence—we won't be able to keep the change hidden from view. Our kids will see it. They'll know it's not an act. And they'll be changed by it as well.

The day I shared my testimony for the first time with my kids, I tried my best to describe for them what the Lord had shown me about myself, what I was seeking to change and repent of, what I was trying to do in response to this blast of spiritual conviction I'd been given—things such as spending more time in Bible study, committing to a greater freedom in sharing my faith with others, becoming a more deliberate leader at home as a husband and father. "Aw, that's great, Dad; that's nice, Dad," was basically their response. I was doing all the talking, and they were doing a lot of nodding.

Then they said, "You know what we've seen you doing different already?"

"No, what?" I was almost afraid to ask. And sure enough, out of all the goal-oriented changes I'd written down and pledged to pursue, the one thing they were about to mention wasn't anything I'd even thought of or been pondering over.

"We've noticed you singing in church," they said.

"Huh?"

"You used to not sing much during worship. You mostly just stood there. But now you're singing. Like you're into it. We've noticed that."

Well, I don't really know *what* they saw. I didn't even realize I was singing more or less during the worship service than at any time prior to that. And if they call what I do "singing," they obviously don't know a whole lot about what singing even is.

But that's just how God works. When He starts to prune us and refine us in certain areas, fresh fruit starts growing out all over the place. Even in places we didn't even notice it was growing. And before we know what's happening, the testimonies we're *living* are becoming much more compelling to our kids, our families, and others than any old testimony we could only *talk* about.

HOME FIRES

Jesus' final declaration of mission to His disciples, just before departing the earth, was that they wait for His Father to deliver on a promise: the gift of the Holy Spirit. And once they'd received the enabling power that was sure to come from that transaction, they were to consider themselves both commissioned and equipped to "be my witnesses in Jerusalem, and in all Judea and Samaria, and to the ends of the earth" (Acts 1:8). That's a bold vision.

And while this "ends of the earth" mandate has sparked the church into creating entire mission movements and humanitarian initiatives and global organizations with multimillion-dollar budgets, the hometown piece of this program—the Jerusalem part—has often failed to generate the same amount of buzz and interest. For instance, we can get people signed up to go to Honduras and New Delhi on friends-and-family-funded mission trips, but we can't get them to go next door to get to know their neighbors.

Or, to say it another way, we'll take our kids to church every week in hopes they'll hear what they need to know about Jesus, but we won't tell them much about Jesus on all the other days of the week when they're right there under our roofs.

Now, I'm not meaning to pick; I've done the same thing. I know how it happens. I understand the discomfort and awkwardness we're trying to avoid by playing it safer, by seeking to do our evangelism with more institutional expertise and efficiency. But we're missing a huge blessing by not keeping the gospel a living, breathing reality among our families. The simple interchange of personal testimony is one of the key drivers in bringing this blessing home, as a means to both our children's salvation as well as their (and our) continued growth and experience with the Lord.

I realize, now, when the topic turns toward our kids' salvation, we parents tend to get a little nervous. We don't want to force anything. We don't want to be manipulative in any way. We know that, in some cases, conversion to Christ is an immediate, emotional moment of awareness and surrender. In other cases, a person's walk into faith can be more of a process that grows and builds a bit at a time, moving more steadily and seamlessly toward Christ, rather than the result of some kind of spiritual explosion. What, then, are we supposed to be looking for? How do we know? What do we need to be sure we hear them say? What if they don't really understand what they're doing?

Hey. Remember what I told you I'd determined my one thing in life was to be? "To make Christ known to my kids." Not to *save* them. Not to *convert* them. Simply to *make Christ known* to them. The Bible tells me "neither the one who plants nor the one who waters is anything, but only God, who makes things grow" (1 Cor. 3:7). Or as Jesus said, "No one can come to me unless the Father who sent me draws them" (John 6:44). So I don't see any biblical reason for thinking I can script my children's faith and determine exactly how or when they're supposed to bow their knee to Jesus. That's not my job. But I see *all kinds* of biblical reasons for believing that God can do anything He wants to do in my kids' lives and hearts, all by Himself. My job is simply to cooperate with Him, faithfully sharing the truth with them, not fretful or afraid that I'm going to mess up His plans if I do something wrong or fail to pick up on a certain cue.

There's some amazing freedom in that.

The freedom just to share. The freedom of being sure you're doing the right thing. The freedom to sit back and watch—and to *know*—God is going to draw those children uniquely to Himself in accordance with the plans He eternally had in mind when He created them.

Let me tell you how I know this. When we shared our testimony with our kids—who were preteens and a teenager at the time—I'd also asked them to prepare their own personal testimonies, based on those three simple markers: their life before Christ, how they met Christ, and their life after meeting Christ. Nothing fancy, just whatever they wanted to share.

I knew my kids pretty well, of course, same as you know yours. Or I *thought* I knew. I'd have guessed I could probably write out their personal testimonies for them and be fairly close to accurate. We had experienced one another's various high and low spots together, so I expected to hear mainly a ten- or twelve- or sixteen-year-old rehash of stuff I already knew.

Nope. And it was the most awesome thing Wanda and I had ever heard—not because they were so eloquent or polished in their delivery but because we were learning things about our kids we'd never known. Memories. Moments. Private little windows they'd experienced where God had opened Himself up to them, captured their attention, revealed little nuggets of truth to them in ways that were so personal and delicate and powerful and riveting. He hadn't always done it how I thought He'd done it. But here they were, telling me, "Yeah, that's how He did it."

I hadn't even known. Perhaps, in fact, *they* hadn't really known or hadn't really pieced it all together until they were challenged to think of it as a story. *Their* story. But now they have it, just as I have mine, just as my wife has hers. The story of how God made Himself real . . . to *us*. The most important story we can ever tell. And every one of those stories is a living, ongoing, developing picture of how God did what God does: seeks and saves the lost. And we get to be part of that. What an indescribable privilege. Not just at the ends of the earth, but right here in the middle of our own living rooms.

EARTH SHATTERING

Paul and his missionary friend Silas were trying to keep their spirits up in a Philippian prison around midnight one night (Acts 16:25–34), singing and praying. They could've been moping and complaining. But not Paul, of course. Which doesn't surprise us. It's kind of what we've come to expect of him. Just like we almost could have expected what happened next—a violent earthquake that struck amid the darkness, enough to rattle the doors off their hinges and create all the conditions for a massive jailbreak.

Heads can roll when things like this happen, even if the people responsible for maintaining order can point to unavoidable circumstances as the main cause. So when the jailer, jarred awake, looked around and realized what was happening, he lunged at the first reflex of a man in his position—a public official facing mass hysteria on his watch and certain punishment in his future. He drew his sword with the intention of running himself through.

"Wait!" Paul shouted above the rumble. "Don't harm yourself! We are all here!"

The jailer, who probably within the past hour had been cursing this very singing prisoner for disturbing his sleep, now rushed toward the sound of that same voice, falling to the ground, all in a tremble, crying, "Sirs, what must I do to be saved?"

This guy now had a testimony. And between the expectation of Paul ("Believe in the Lord Jesus, and you will be saved—you and your household") and the fearful desperation of this prison warden, the next thing that happened—"immediately"—was a mad dash home to tell his wife and kids what had happened. And to tell them about this Jesus. Before it was too late.

I'm guessing the earth's not literally shaking under your feet right now, the way it was shaking under that man in his midnight moment of crisis. You have stuff to do. You have life to live. You have calls to make. You have business to take care of. But what if something were to happen to you? What if a situation or accident arose where you didn't know how many more opportunities you'd be given to communicate eye to eye with your spouse, your kids, your family? Would you worry you had left out some vital, valuable things you had intended to talk about with them, to be sure they heard from you? Would this last chance slip away before you told them the single most important story in your life?

I don't know. Only *you* know.

But I'd like to suggest that the ground is shaking a little more than it probably feels. Time gets away more quickly than we think. And God has brought you to this place in your life—as He did the Philippian jailer—where your focus now is more intently turned toward your family and the spiritual development of their hearts. No more than that government official, after living through what he'd experienced, would've kept the story to himself and not shared it with the people who lived at his house, you don't need to be shy about telling your story either. It's the most important story you can tell. And your family needs to hear it.

I'm not talking about a double-spaced treatise with expressive vocabulary and literary quality. I'm not talking about an hour-long ramble over every pothole and detail. This story is simply you. It's yours. And while you may not have ever sat down to try putting it together into an encapsulated whole, this familiar story with both yours and God's fingerprints all over it is a powerful tool at your command. Just ask the jailer in Acts 16 who was "filled with joy because he had come to believe in God—he and his whole household" (v. 34). A story of faith is a powerful thing. And sharing it can become a groundbreaking moment in your family's life.

CHAPTER 7

WHO? WHAT? HOW?

Step 3: Define Your Values, Your Vision, Your Mission

The part that makes our individual testimonies so fascinating is that while each one centers on a single nucleus—a personal relationship with Jesus Christ—every story is still entirely unique. *It's our own.* No two of these spiritual journeys— just as no two snowflakes or fingerprints or Sunday morning political talk show opinions—are ever quite the same.

Our families are like that too. Many things are similar between us, general patterns of makeup and composition that are common to most every home. Yet each of our families still bears its own distinctiveness—in its background and spiritual legacy (as we've seen), personal experience (as we've seen), and the nature of our values and priorities (as we're about to see). We may be much the same, and yet we're different.

For instance, I'm sure you want your kids to be healthy, happy, and successful at what they strive to do and accomplish. *Same as all of us.* I'm sure you want them to receive a quality education, to be afforded every opportunity for maximizing their potential and for making the most of their various gifts and abilities. *Same as all of us.* I'm sure you want them to enjoy good friendships and relationships, doing life with people who are encouraging and supportive, people who bring out the best in them, instead of leading them astray into trouble and error. And as believers in Christ, of course, you want them to be faithful followers who live by the teachings of His Word and who experience throughout their lifetimes a satisfying closeness with Him as they flesh out their own callings and serve others in His name. *Same as all of us.* We share many common goals and values.

But here's what happens. As long as we're content to float along with these generic hopes and labels, without any more specific, focused awareness of what drives us as a family—what inspires us, what unites us, what fulfills God's uniquely designed purpose for our children and our marriage—we leave ourselves open to chaos and confusion. To the whims of outside influences and the clutter of overcrowded schedules and commitments. To the vain attempt of trying to be everything to everybody. And, therefore, not truly being ourselves and not building into our kids an anchored sense of identity, home, and direction.

So I hope you see—as I begin talking about the importance of knowing your *values*, of having a *vision*, and then letting it all develop into a *mission* for your family—that the scope of what this process can create in you goes far beyond just spiritual things, beyond merely what happens on family devotional night. *I'm talking about life.* I'm talking about parents like you who really want to guide your family well, who want to make solid decisions in terms of your children's activities and future and areas of focus. You want to be sure you're leading them wisely toward a clear destination, that you're seeking out and saying yes to things that move you closer to where you're wanting to go as a family, all while defending yourselves against detours and distractions that can only lead you further off course or unnecessarily delay the trip.

You may be driving the best you can, the best you know how, as I'm sure you are. But if you haven't thought through your values and written them down, you're always just guessing. You're playing hunches. Navigating by feel. That makes it much more likely you'll miss a turn someplace, probably at the worst possible time, when everybody's counting on you to know where you're going.

I'm assuming you've already tried it that way, as I have. And I'm assuming you're tired of it, as I was. Tired of trusting that your own reflexes and snap judgments will somehow be enough to keep you landing on your feet, instead of leading out with the steady consistency of someone who knows what your family is truly all about—leading with a *vision*, leading on a *mission*.

It all starts with knowing your values.

VALUABLE LESSON

For six full weeks beginning in September 1982—long before the days when terrorist activity had become a sadly expected intrusion into modern life—all three major television networks led off their evening newscasts with the latest details surrounding seven mysterious poisoning deaths in the American Midwest. It was a national scare with chilling possibilities. As time wore on, despite being unable to locate the person responsible for the deadly attacks (a case that remains unsolved to this day), investigators were at least able to succeed at isolating the culprit's sinister murder weapon: cyanide-laced capsules of Extra-Strength Tylenol, traced back to customer purchases at five different Chicago-area stores.

Perhaps, even if you're old enough to remember this happening at all, it's become one of those vague memories that shows up every now and then or every decade as an "On This Date" entry, one of those quick mentions of historical trivia. That's probably the fuzzy way I'd remember it myself, except that my job at the time, fresh out of college, was as a sales rep servicing food stores and drugstores in Chicago, where all seven of those poisonings had taken place. In fact, one of the stores where the tainted medicine had been bought was in my territory. And my employer? McNeil Consumer Products Company, a subsidiary of Johnson & Johnson.

MAKERS OF TYLENOL

I couldn't believe what I was in the middle of. I wasn't even on staff long enough to have gone through formal training yet. I was twenty-one years old, three months on the job, thrust into a situation that now required me to interact with the presidents of huge mass-merchandising companies that supplied local retailers with our products and work as part of a team fielding daily calls from those seeking information about how we were going to deal with this crisis of epic business and societal proportions.

So I remember it all. Frighteningly well. If the panic of the general public was enough to significantly affect their buying habits, making some of them want to empty the shelves in their bathroom medicine cabinets, the intensity raging around those of us at the epicenter of the ordeal was seriously all-consuming. It was all we did. For weeks.

But the memory of those days that has left the most lasting impression on me—as well as on generations of business observers who now consider Johnson & Johnson's successful handling of the situation a case study in how companies should respond to catastrophic events—was the actions of James Burke, Johnson & Johnson's president and CEO.

And it all began with our values.

Walk into Johnson & Johnson corporate headquarters in Brunswick, New Jersey, and one of the first things you'll see in the lobby is a large stone display, almost like a national monument, etched with the words of a vision statement that's been around since the company's inception. It speaks of a four-pronged responsibility to (a) their customers, (b) their employees, (c) their communities, and (d) their shareholders—in that order. And in case that's too much to remember, they boil it all down into a simple and memorable credo that cuts across everything they do as an organization: "We put the needs and well-being of the people we serve first."

While the crisis facing the Johnson & Johnson brand, and certainly Tylenol's market share, held the potential to set back either one's sustainability for the foreseeable future—perhaps forever—and while the decisions required of the corporate leadership were the kind that can spell doom to entire careers, even if undertaken with the full agreement and support of their team of advisers, the man in charge of leading his company through this unprecedented emergency felt as though the hardest calls were actually quite easy to make. In many ways, they'd already been made. By the power of a plan. By the strength and clarity of the company's values and vision. If Johnson & Johnson's stated purpose—as the motto said—was to treat people's needs and well-being as primary, then the choice of what to do next was fairly clear. Difficult to implement, to be sure, but not to decide on what to do.

I remember being on a multi-person conference call with James Burke when someone asked him the obvious question: "How much is this going to cost?" The answer to that question, if he'd felt like giving it, was somewhere north of $100 million— including the recall of more than thirty-one million bottles of Tylenol in circulation; the issuing of store credits to outlets that carried the product; the retooling of machinery in order to switch production from capsules to solid caplets, as well as the industry's first-ever rollout of safety-sealed, tamper-proof packaging; not to mention legal, publicity, and other damage control costs. But the financial answer wasn't up for discussion that day, only the short answer, which went something like this: "I don't ever want to hear the money question coming up again. This is not a money issue; it's an issue of doing the right thing and putting people first."

Values drove the decision.

And *your* values can do the same thing. They can serve the same purpose. They can help you steer the spiritual, relational, and missional direction of your family, while also giving your spouse and kids a GPS for keeping their personal lives on target, helping them stay balanced and aligned along a consistent standard. Values form the nonnegotiable foundation underneath your family that determines who you are, what you want to do, and how you intend to go about doing it.

So what *are* they? What does your family value?

VALUE JUDGMENTS

Values are the things your family considers special and important. They're your priorities. Your points of emphasis. They're the kinds of things for which you make yourself "unbusy" in order to make time to experience, enjoy, and get better at doing.

As you work together to define and rank the values you share as a family, here are a few guidelines that may be helpful:

1. Some of them—the most essential ones—are core, eternal values. We will talk about other kinds of values, but the ones that are most important to embrace and embody are those values we derive from Scripture, which, according to Matthew 6:20, are like "treasures in heaven." They contribute toward our spiritual growth and development. They outlive us in importance and significance. They help us cooperate with what God is trying to accomplish in us, making us more like Him in character, in service, in generosity, and in love.

In my family's case, we've concluded that (1) prayer, (2) worship, and (3) the reading of God's Word are essential values we always want to be pouring ourselves into as individuals and as a group. In all the years we've been doing our biweekly devotional times as a family, these three values are what create the framework for how we spend those moments together. Prayer—always prayer. Worship—always worship. The Word—always the Word. These three things, we believe, will continually keep us growing more in love with God, more humbled by His mercy, more knowledgeable of His ways, and more prepared to share His good news with others. But it's much more than just that.

Since *prayer* is one of our intentional family values, we've developed a written prayer that each of us prays every day, one that is rooted in Scripture and memorized, that keeps us united in focus and purpose. We want prayer to be our lifestyle, our lifeblood, so we stake a lot of importance to it. Since *worship* is another of our family values, we put a great deal of emphasis on church membership and involvement, on regular attendance and frequent worship experienced with fellow believers. And since *God's Word* is also of supreme value to us, we hold each other accountable for reading it and being in it on a daily basis. Regular, planned encounters with God in Scripture are of significant importance in helping us live out what He's placed us on this earth to do, in making ourselves a living sacrifice of obedient gratitude to Him for the grace He's given us.

And, I'm sure, as you seek His direction, as you begin to more clearly formulate how your relationship with Christ is meant to make its most direct impact and influence on your family's identity, you'll be able to crystallize—from the wide choice of noble, biblical values available—the ones that belong at the core of your family, the ones you can grow to champion and encourage together.

2. **Some essential values are ones you don't yet value.** This became really clear to us, especially to me, as we began knocking around what we most prized and emphasized as a family. Things such as the faithful study of God's Word sounded great and all, and we knew it should be one of our highest priorities as Christians. But it wasn't. Not in practice. And that's okay. In fact, to recognize failure as an honest admission is actually a good place to begin, as opposed to what our Enemy wants it to be—the place where we throw up our hands and say we're just not cut out for this.

One of the greatest drawbacks and hindrances to this

discovery exercise—something I always urge people to be watchful for—is the tendency to write down what we think we *should* value without being honest with each other about what we really *do* value. I realize, of course, people aren't trying to plead perfection. That isn't the intention. But if we lay out an ideal that probably isn't very descriptive of what is actually going on, it paints an unrealistic picture that likely only discourages us going forward.

The idea of *pursuing* certain values, of course, is a good thing—a *great* thing—and we ought to challenge one another to yield ourselves to God in those areas where we want to see growth. But our families are works in progress, and our best chance at beginning to exemplify these desired values is to admit how we've been resisting some of them. They'll never really be ours, these values, until we let God imprint and implant them on our hearts as we give His Spirit room and opportunity to change us from the inside out. And this only starts when we come as we are, with no pretense, with no inclination to impress, and we simply say, "Lord, I want this to matter to me, and to us, more than it currently does. Have mercy on us and help us." That's the kind of spirit He loves responding to.

3. Your values can incorporate every facet of life. Of equal concern as the family who overdoes it a tad in compiling their list of values is the family who figures the only ones that qualify (the only ones we're looking for) are Christian-y-sounding things. In the same way as being honest about ourselves and our true priorities is imperative to this process, we should also feel spared of the pressure to artificially act as though God is not interested, for example, in your six-year-old son expressing how much he values playing baseball or how your nine-year-old daughter says she values making good grades. Sports and education may not, in and of themselves, be what we consider "eternal values," but a biblical understanding of God and life means that every undertaking is an opportunity (as the *Westminster Confession of Faith* says) "to glorify God and enjoy him forever."

So as you think through what your family loves and what gives you your own distinct identity, don't be shy about valuing things such as hospitality, competition, excellence, and healthy debate or the open expression of opinions and ideas, scientific discovery and curiosity, nutrition and fitness, outdoor play and exercise, summer vacations and holiday traditions.

All of these are values. They help cement your distinct identity. They may or may not come with their own prescribed chapter and verse from the Bible, but they do fall under the biblical admonition and invitation that says, "Whatever you do, work at it with all your heart, as working for the Lord, not for human masters," because you know it is always "the Lord Christ you are serving" (Col. 3:23–24), no matter where or how you're serving Him.

4. Values are timeless, not temporary. A big part of what goes into developing a vision for your children is seeing them not merely as whatever age kids they happen to be at the moment. As parents, we need to already be envisioning them as the twenty-year-olds and thirty-year-olds they will one day become. I'm not talking about growing them up before they're ready. (The world and culture are already way too busy doing *that*.) But how will these values of yours—these values of *theirs* as part of your family—help shape them as they move into adulthood? That's what you're going for: growing lifelong disciples.

One of the values of Scripture, for instance, that has always struck us as being crucially important is the idea of not being "yoked together with unbelievers" (2 Cor. 6:14), especially in terms of the marriage relationship. This obviously wasn't a pressing matter when our kids were ten, twelve, and fourteen. But since this biblical concept is one we knew would one day be instrumental in the kind of life choices they'd make, we deliberately introduced this idea to them in stages along the way. The sanctity of marriage vows and the importance of raising children in a Christian home are values we wanted to instill in them as they were growing up, along with some of the scriptural teaching that would enable these commitments to become reality in their lives down the line.

So not only are the values you're defining today a key component in how you're leading your family at present; not only are these the values you want to deepen and intensify in one another through ongoing practice and experience; not only do these values touch on every kind of endeavor in which you and your kids participate; but they also assist you in helping to shape your children into the men and women they will become.

This one thing—knowing your values—can solve so many of the concerns you've been feeling about why you're not leading your family as you should or as you want. It will help you do it better. It's what could transform you into a dad or mom who is becoming more and more effective each year and each season in tapping in to your kids' hearts. Knowing and prioritizing your family's core values can help you accomplish so much.

It's what gives your family its vision.

VISION

Why do you think God, in Isaiah 6, gave His reluctant prophet a vision of Himself "high and exalted, seated on a throne," where the train of His robe "filled the temple" (v. 1)? Why did God reveal to him angels with six wings, worshiping at such high volume that the doorposts of the throne room began to shake and the whole place filled with smoke as one of these creatures flew down and touched Isaiah's lips with a live coal from the altar, declaring his sins forgiven, commissioning him to bold service as a spokesman of the Lord?

Why such a vision? Why be so descriptive and detailed?

And why did God give the apostle John, exiled on the island of Patmos, a vision of the risen Christ? A vision of a seven-sealed scroll that only the slain Lamb was able to open? A vision of a furious Enemy persecuting God's people, only, ultimately, to be conquered and destroyed for all time? A vision of the ushering in of a new heaven and a new earth, with a new Jerusalem coming down "prepared as a bride beautifully dressed for her husband" (Rev. 21:2), where the people of God will be safe in His presence forever and ever?

Why a vision? Why did God create us to respond to vision?

What's so important about having a vision for your family?

Tell you what, if *vision* feels like too airy of a word, just think of it as a *mental image* of what you want your family to be. When you're reading God's Word, when you're pondering what He desires for you, your marriage, and your children, what does that image look like to you? See, I believe you already have one. Though you perhaps haven't tried capturing it and solidifying it, I think a general picture image of what you want for your children and family is already in your head. Trouble is, it may be like that big boilerplate of hopes and dreams I gave you at the beginning of this chapter. The picture image may be all jumbled up in a haze of commonly accepted expectations that kind of settle around us as parents without our really even thinking about it—all those typical things we're supposed to want to see happen in our children's lives.

But in order to lead your family in the direction God is specifically trying to take you, through your values, your family needs a statement of vision from you to give you something to rally around and shoot for—a vision that will keep drawing your family back, like a magnet, to its roots and core purpose. Just as John's vision gave his readers and himself a realistic sense of hope and inspiration to endure the challenges they were going through—just as it gave them an image of future generations coming along in the wake of their faith and trust in God's plan for the ages—your vision for your family will help everyone see that God is actually taking your family somewhere special as you live out life together. It's the part *your* family is meant to play as a vital part of *His* family.

Vision statements. If the thought of sitting down to craft a brief vision statement for your family makes you suddenly eager to go out and clean the garage or do some other menial task you've been putting off all season, trust me, you're in good company. I can appreciate the avoidance, the diversionary tactics. But I assure you, if that's the case, you're viewing this job as being harder and more painful than it really is.

Hey. You're not drafting the Magna Carta or the Declaration of Independence. There's no right or wrong statement. There's only *your* statement—your way of expressing, in as few words as possible, what you want to see your family become by God's grace and power. Think of it like this: Your list of values helps define who you are. And when armed with a more concrete grasp of *who you are*, your vision statement can now describe *what you hope to accomplish* as you live out those values.

So start there. With your values. Write them down. Take them into prayer with you. Ask God to help you reduce this vital information about what you, your family, and His Word deem to be important into a single statement that pulls all of it together into a compact carrying size.

Again, it doesn't need to be Christian-speak. Doesn't need to blow people away with your grasp of the language. It just needs to be yours. It needs to reflect what your family is all about and what you, as the spiritual leader, sense to be the main purpose for why God has put you all together in this fashion, at this time, with this background, with these values, and with a fresh new desire for every single one of you to be directly in the middle of His will.

Vision guides the way for *everything*.

I'm not going to tell you what our vision statement is. I'm always afraid that if I do, I'll send people in a direction they wouldn't have gone otherwise. It's not because I'm uncomfortable with our vision statement, nor is it because our statement is any more special than anybody else's. It's just ours. Yours will be different. But I will tell you what I've said before: even though our vision statement is no more than a couple dozen words, I've backed it down into a four-word motto that simply says "Unity in the Spirit." This, in a nutshell, is what I want for us. It's what my wife, my kids, and I always need to fight for and maintain in order to steward our faith well and keep it continuing into future generations. Unity in the Spirit is our family's *what*. It's what we're going for. Always. In everything.

As is true of every family, we have our challenges. We have our disagreements. Small, medium, and large. We have the occasional breakdown in communication, when one or another of us fails to understand what somebody else means or is trying to do. We're a long way from having it all together, I can assure you.

We've had this vision in place for many years. And on those once-in-a-while days when I've been upset about something, just not feeling like getting along with anybody, our family vision has often been the thing that has held me in check and brought me back to my senses. On nights when one or more of our kids may not be in the mood for our family phone call because they're personally dealing with something at home or they've gotten crossways with a sibling (or a father!), they still keep jumping on that line, week after week, year after year. They're called back to it by our vision: Unity in the Spirit.

I can think of more than one situation through the years where—again, like everybody—we were wrestling with a family issue that easily could have escalated into something that sent us off to our respective camps and opposite corners. But because we had a vision that we all had agreed to embrace ahead of time, I was able to say, "Guys, we've got to stay unified in the Spirit here. We don't have to agree on everything, but whichever way this plays out, we still need to be unified, all right?"

That's what a vision can do. It's like glue. It keeps us all held in place, where we belong. This vision you establish is not just words on paper. It's a living message. It's something you can keep trotting out, in the middle of any crisis or decision moment, and lay it down like a yardstick or a carpenter's level, just to remind one another, "This is who we are, and this is what we've promised to be and do—for one another, for our Lord, and for the generations who need us to be standing strong, long after we've forgotten what this little conflict was all about."

Claim your vision. Put it in writing. It's one of the greatest gifts you'll ever give your family.

Values. They're who you are.

Vision. It's what you want to do and be.

MISSION

It's time now to get it all moving. To crank the engine. To put gas on the fire the Lord's been building. To start assembling a rocket ship on this launchpad, this solid slab of groundwork, where you and your family can begin turning all these well-placed nouns into real action verbs.

Everybody needs a *mission*. And that's what you're about to give your family. A *how* that can go along with the *who* and the *what*.

I realize—even though I'm imagining you itching to start shifting into action mode—a tinge of doubt can often persist, a bit of uncertainty or unsettledness about how to transform your values and vision into a workable mission statement. But allow me again to try to peel the pressure off because, as with everything we seek to do in obedience to God's Word, our main job is just to show up willing to work. He's the One, really, who does all the heavy lifting.

I remember, for example, when we first started talking to our kids about what they valued and what was important to them, a steady theme kept cropping up that, honestly, I'd never realized we shared. Granted, our children were a little bit older at the time than yours may be, but the same principle and expectation still apply. The proof became quite obvious that God had been working in every one of our kids, as well as in Wanda and me, to give each of us a genuine passion for what I've come to call "the lost and the least"—those who are hurting, those who are suffering from material deficiencies and lack but also, most important, from their need for a Savior in Christ Jesus. While I wasn't sure in the moment what that really meant, the Lord sure seemed to be saying He wanted this value to become not just an interesting observation but also an intentional mission. A distinctive factor in how our family functions.

That's why today, not only is our family committed to helping other families experience the unity that grows from being devoted to in-home discipleship; not only is our family committed to systematically growing in the Word; not only is our family serious about helping one another live a life that's worthy of the calling we've received as God's children; we're also diligent in staying equipped and watchful for opportunities to share our faith through personal witnessing and to share our time and resources with those in need.

Neither I nor my family would ever have been able to figure all of this out on our own. This wasn't simply the whiteboard summary and spillover of a scheduled brainstorming meeting. This came from knowing—like you—that God had led me to take a bold step toward assuming spiritual leadership in my family and then turning it over to Him to fill in the blanks, when blanks were all I really had to offer.

He'll do the same with you. I promise. He'll help you tie

together whatever loose ends seem to be dangling disconnectedly from your family's collection of values, showing you how to shape them all into not only a clear vision statement for *what* He wants your family to accomplish but also a clear mission statement for *how* you can go out there and actually accomplish it. The *vision* is where you want to go; the *mission* is how you get there.

But—please don't miss this—the most important element in how you get to your vision statement and your mission statement is that you go there on the altar. In prayer, repentance, and pleading. Don't worry so much about what it says or how quickly you're able to complete it. Everything can always be reworked, reworded, or readjusted later, as many times as you feel the need. The much bigger issue—bigger than *who* you determine you are, bigger than *what* you decide to do, even bigger than *how* you choose to implement it all—is *where* you are when you reach these conclusions.

Do it on the altar of surrender. Of faith, of trust, of worship. Do it in the stolen quiet of moments with God when you can really be sure He's got your full attention. Do it with no other motive than wanting His absolute best for your family and your children, remaining fully dependent on Him to lead you well so you can become His kind of leader in your home.

Do it in humble, believing trust. And He will begin to do some amazing things in you. In *all* of you.

CHAPTER 8

INTENTIONS IN ACTION

Step 4: Set Your Goals

What is the first thing bankers would say to us if we tried to secure funding for a small business we wanted to start? "Let's see your business plan."

What do you want to do? Who are you trying to reach? What's your vision? What's your mission?

They have a right to know, don't they? Why should they and their depositors invest anything in our bright ideas if all those ideas are in our heads but we can't explain them, not only to the investor but also to the potential customers and clients we're hoping to capture? While *we* may be willing to risk somebody else's money solely on the optimism of what we think our dreams are worth, *they* want to see results of concrete thinking about how and why a product or service meets a need in the marketplace and whether our image of success has its basis in sound logic. Right?

We would expect nothing less. We wouldn't dream of the loan officer just reaching into his top drawer, handing us a form and a pen, and asking, "How much do you want?" We may not personally possess the financial means to go out there and start conducting commerce on our own. But nobody would be doing us any favor, truly, by throwing money at our entrepreneurial hunches if we haven't first shown a willingness and a desire to invest what we do have—*ourselves*—into figuring out who we are, what we want to accomplish, and how we want to accomplish it.

That's not being mean. That's just being wise. By requiring something of us, by expecting our cooperation, that's how the one who holds the ability to bless and empower our efforts helps ensure we're operating with wisdom.

So if the practical, spiritual process involved in tightening down your family's values, vision, and mission feels like a burdensome chore, one that's sure to grind all the fun out of this journey, that's not what it's there for at all. Don't think of God as sitting across the desk from you, looking over the top of His glasses, staring you into discomfort while you sweat and squirm, forced to answer His questions and meet His prerequisites or else walk out empty-handed. God, the Bible tells us, is a generous giver (James 1:5): "He rewards those who earnestly seek him" (Heb. 11:6). He gives to those who ask and seek and knock (Matt. 7:7). If we think *we* know how to give good gifts to our children, "how much more will your Father in heaven give good gifts to those who ask him!" (v. 11). He is a sower of seed (Luke 8:5). He loves planting new things in kingdom soil, of which your home and family meet all the criteria.

But He wants that seed to grow. He wants it landing in good soil:

- **Surrendered** soil that's receptive and open to new possibilities.
- **Humble** soil that's been tilled up and turned over.

- **Dependent** soil that's continually being cared for, nourished, and watered.
- **Sacrificed** soil that gives all the glory for what grows there to God alone.

Therefore, He calls us to the win-win of wisdom. To the development of plans that maximize our potential for expansion. To the exhilaration of active growth opportunities. And to hearts that truly live to share the bounty of all this spiritual production with the people we care about the most. By working with surrendered, humble, dependent, and self-sacrificial parents, He can make new, exciting growth start happening all around us, in everything we touch, our children becoming like "well-nurtured plants" sprouting up around our tables (Ps. 144:12), while our hearts, our marriages, our families, and all our personal endeavors in work, service, and ministry are brimming over with evidence of the increase.

That's why we're doing all this. *That's* why the prayerful effort of discovering our values, vision, and mission is so worth it.

And that's why we keep offering Him all our needs and weaknesses so He can transform them into positives and strengths. We throw open the door for Him to plant Himself ever deeper into our lives and in the lives of our children.

By setting goals.

MILE MARKERS

If *vision* establishes the destination you want to reach and if *mission* defines the path that takes you there, *goals* are the milestones that measure your progress. They don't make you *more* saved or *less* saved. They don't give your family *more* status or *less* status. They just help keep you motivated and determined to become everything you possibly can be for Him—and able to celebrate and worship Him for the specific, recognizable ways He does it.

The alternative is to perpetually underachieve: To whine about why we're not experiencing any more joy in our relationship with Christ. To wonder why church and most every other spiritual undertaking is so lifeless and boring. And to revert to a judgmental, put-down attitude toward other people and families who obviously are exaggerating about the remarkable way God works in their lives because we know for a fact that most of what we pray for and hear preached about is wishful thinking at best. It doesn't really change much of what goes on in real life for the rest of the workweek.

That's the way it can seem when we reduce our family's experiences with God to an unexamined, undisciplined level, where we're following Him only by feelings. Nowhere else in life would we expect to see measurable results from such a haphazard approach. But somehow we deceive ourselves into believing that spiritual growth and progress in our faith ought to happen just because we want it to happen. God ought to hand it out like trick-or-treat candy simply because we dressed up for it, came over, and looked the part.

Well, what if we stopped working so hard just to look the part? What if we became genuinely invested in wanting to know Christ more intimately and serve Him more passionately? What if we determined not to instill in our kids the implied impression that He doesn't really deserve our best? What if we began deliberately aligning the way we think so it matches up with the way the Bible defines truth, so by devoting ourselves to Christ and His Word, we and our families would naturally begin bearing "much fruit" (John 15:5)?

Yes, noticeable fruit.

God already tells us what will happen if we do. A verse I've already mentioned: "He who began a good work in you will carry it on to completion until the day of Christ Jesus" (Phil. 1:6). He is so invested in wanting to equip and empower your family and mine to achieve our goals that He has promised to keep us moving forward as we actively participate with Him.

So let's get on our work clothes, work gloves, and work boots. Let's pull out our garden tools, our spiritual rakes and shovels. And let's put ourselves in position for the Sower to come help us harvest a crop, right here where we live—not only this season but also the next season and the next, even (by God's grace) into the next generations.

GOAL TENDING

I hope you know me well enough by now, having read this far, to know I'm not here to tell you what to do. I'm not some kind of spiritual whiz who's figured out what everybody's been missing all these years when it comes to family discipleship. And even if I was, it wouldn't mean I had all the answers. I'm just an average guy trying to hold it all together. No way do I think I have it all together. But I do believe the Bible paints a reliable pathway all of us would do well to travel in seeking to grow in Christ, as well as in helping our children grow in Christ. I'm not saying it's confined to a single color scheme that can't be adapted to your family's particular style. Remember, the idea to keep in mind when you're leading your kids spiritually is to envision how this is preparing them to be nineteen-year-old college kids, twenty-nine-year-old parents, and thirty-nine-year-old leaders in their churches, businesses, and homes and families. You're building long term, not just looking for nice little service projects you think your seven-year-old might learn something from as well as enjoy this weekend.

So I suggest that your first goal as a family not be an outing to feed the homeless. That's a fantastic goal, a very biblical goal for your family to be working toward. But listen: many people feel sympathetic toward ministering to the homeless and to others in obvious need, whether they actually end up doing it or not—whether they're even Christians or not, right? All I'm saying is that before you run out with your kids to the homeless shelter, before you turn a pang of guilt into a bunch of twelve-packs of Gatorade, seek to understand, as a family, why the gospel would motivate you to do something like that. You and I can raise a generation of compassionate kids who turn out to be activists. But what we need to be raising up is a generation of believers who realize that what they do for the hungry, the thirsty, the sick, and the stranger, they're doing for the Lord Jesus Himself (Matt. 25:34–40). That's how ongoing acts of service create a lasting ripple effect that not only ministers aid to the hurting but also inspires even greater acts of service throughout a family, throughout the years.

When Jesus called His first disciples, He laid before them a vision of going out and "catching men" for God's redemptive purposes, just as some of them had been in the business of catching fish for a living (Luke 5:1–11). But Christ's chosen way of growing these men toward the point where they were ready to become *martyrs* for the gospel was by inviting them to come walk with Him, a preparatory process that went on for somewhere between two to three years. He knew they needed to see some things and learn some things before they just shot off being heroes. Otherwise, they'd never really grasp the purpose for why they were doing it. And, more important, they'd never be able to sustain it.

For this reason I see wisdom in orienting our family's goals along a similar trajectory. I feel as though the Scripture backs me up on this, and I know for sure I've watched it have a meaningful effect in my children's lives, not only as kids but also as they have grown into adulthood. So again, while I'm not prescribing that you adopt my method or else be doomed to sailing hopelessly off track, I do believe molding this plan to fit your family will prove to be a confident, long-lasting way of seeing some solid spiritual dividends pay off for decades to come.

I tend to need easy ways of remembering things, so I've organized my goal-thinking around three main pillars:

- *Connection*
- *Commitment*
- *Commission*

Each year we focus our family's goals around only one of these main emphases, approaching them in a three-year cycle and in this particular order. Let me show you what I'm talking about.

I. **Connection Goals.** During a Connection year, we set goals that help us make strides in how we grasp basic tenets of the Christian faith and connect them to our lives. We want to learn more about who *God* is, who *we* are, who *Christ* is, what His *truth* is, and what He wants us to *do* as His people and how He calls us to *follow* Him as His disciples. All basic stuff. All biblical stuff. And it all stems from wanting to help my kids (and myself) truly know what the Bible says, to know what they believe, and also begin to own their understanding for *why* they believe it. To make those kinds of connections.

Remember what I told you Wanda said to me on that anniversary trip of ours years ago? Remember what inspired her and my (especially her) initial motivation for why I needed to become more intentional and deliberate in leading our children spiritually? It was this: We didn't want them showing up on a college campus or heading out into the job world not knowing how to defend their faith. We wanted them able to offer compelling, Bible-backed reasons for why they were following Christ, and for why whatever person to whom they were speaking should seriously consider the claims of Scripture.

Well, here you go. That's the underlying reason behind why we've incorporated Connection goals as the leading edge of our family's spiritual plan. I think you'd be wise to start there, too, because I'd be shocked if you didn't share some of the same desires as Wanda and I. But no matter what you foresee as your incentive for offering spiritual direction to your children, it undoubtedly entails what Ephesians 6:4 describes as bringing them up "in the training and instruction of the Lord." Connecting them to biblical truth.

I keep going back to that parable of the sower. The farmer sows the seed. Jesus sows the Word. And as a parent, as a father, I want my kids to know this God—I mean, *really* know this

God—who has acted with such extreme love toward them by revealing everything they need to know about Him through the gift of Holy Scripture. We take them to the Word because He's shared with us the Word; He Himself is the Word. The seeds He's sowing in me, the seeds He's sowing in them—I want to create a natural environment where the Spirit can connect all these things together so that each of us learns and grows, from Him and from one another.

2. Commitment Goals. We're all aware, of course, that just *knowing* is not enough. The seed sown by the farmer in Jesus' parable was scattered across four different types of ground. Same Word, different environments. The opportunity for the soil to soak it up and let it germinate into fruition was available to every piece of land where it was broadcast. But merely having the Word within reach and view doesn't mean it's actually growing within us or our children. We don't want them simply to know it; we want them to live it.

That's the idea behind this particular type of goal, which we create for our family during what we call Commitment years. We seek to identify ways we can allow the Holy Spirit to help us commit to putting embedded principles into emboldened practice. We want to build spiritual momentum and confidence by keeping the dots connected between God's Word and our witness. "Teach me your way, LORD," King David said, "that I may rely on your faithfulness; give me an undivided heart, that I may fear your name" (Ps. 86:11). Consistency in thought and deed. Commitment to living out our beliefs. That's the idea.

We always want to be careful, of course, to keep from fostering any kind of legalistic motive in our kids' (or our) behavior. Christian character development always remains the work of

God in our hearts, and the satisfying contentment we receive as a result is intended as fodder for worship, not as food for our pride and ego. For with the faithful, He proves *Himself* faithful; with the blameless, He shows *Himself* blameless; with the pure, He shows *Himself* pure (Ps. 18:25–26). It's all about Jesus making *His* changes in us.

But what joy we can experience in our homes and personal lives as we more consistently neutralize the impurities and excuses that characterize the unprofitable soil samples from Jesus' story. No longer being so hard, deaf, and resistant to His Spirit. No longer being so shallow and fair-weather that we only obey if it's something simple or if it's immediately advantageous to us. No longer allowing worries and distractions to choke out our top priorities. It's that kind of commitment that will lead us and our kids to respond to His love with Spirit-filled living.

3. Commission Goals. Every third year (according to how we do our plan), we shift the bulk of our focus onto how we can take what we believe, take what we've experienced, and give it away. In service. To others. For the glory of God.

Our Bible studies during these years concentrate primarily on what the Scripture teaches about serving and self-sacrifice. And our goals trail along with the same mentality. For example, we might look for available opportunities through our church to engage in ministry to shut-ins or underprivileged children or some other group of people in our community who need help and who need Jesus. We might look into taking a mission trip with the entire family—rather than just an isolated one or two of us—out of the country to an impoverished area, experiencing both the heartbreak of human need and the hands-on impact of Christ's love, all together with our kids.

And we might focus on feeding and befriending the homeless. But we'd keep reinforcing whatever type of mission God's Spirit was commissioning and leading us to do by letting it bubble up from His Word, from prayer, from what He shows us about why people who've been transformed by Christ are always in the business of helping to transform others.

So between your goals for (1) *connection*—learning about the fundamentals of Christian faith, (2) *commitment*—applying those truths to life by the power of the Holy Spirit, and (3) *commission*—looking beyond yourselves to the physical and spiritual needs of others—imagine the kind of exponential growth you could expect to take place, right in your own family garden. Jesus said it could amount to "thirty, some sixty, some a hundred times what was sown" (Mark 4:20). Measurable progress. Year-after-year results. High yield. Good soil.

That's the power and promise of setting family goals.

WATERING FOR GROWTH

As I shared earlier, I set a goal early in life, inspired by my father and by other life experiences, to impact the culture of corporate America. An admirable goal. Much better than, say, trying to make a million dollars in a hoped-for number of years or to reach some particular level of rank and status in the business world.

My goal was larger and of wider scope than mere personal gain. I meant it, and I was serious about it. Yet it was a temporal goal. Significant, but not eternal. Noble, but not worthy of being number one. I grew to discover how it needed to take its place behind some truly superior goals, such as discovering that my true identity is found in Christ, instead of in my work title or any other job description; investing myself in others, beginning with my wife and children; and promising that everyone the Lord brings into my life for the purpose of hearing the gospel will faithfully hear it from me. These kinds of milestones have given me a new heading, a new north, upon which to affix my navigation system.

I wish I could report to you that I've been excelling in each of these goal areas. Unfortunately, I still have a long way to go. But I can tell you this much: *I've seen changes.* Encouraging changes. Changes in my priorities. Changes in my desires. Changes in where I concentrate my limited span of time and resources. Changes in my sensitivity to the Spirit. I can tell it's slowly developing into a more regular state of watchful anticipation.

God is the One doing it. Through Him and His Word, through ongoing prayer and worship, my understanding of who I am as a new creation in Christ is becoming clearer to me, year by year—just as He's also helping me see my purpose in life more clearly, as well as the way I'm supposed to lead my family. I still have lots of room remaining for growth and improvement, but I'm certainly in dedicated pursuit. I know I'm not the man I used to be, and I'm glad to see that man fading into the distance. And this guy in the mirror today will, hopefully, look paltry and ane-mic in comparison to the one that God, by His grace, will keep transforming in me.

That's simply His promise, to you, to me, to our kids, to all of us. By chasing eternally minded goals with full reliance on the active empowering of the Holy Spirit, He assures us that "the righteous will flourish like a palm tree, they will grow like a cedar of Lebanon; planted in the house of the LORD, they will flourish in the courts of our God. They will still bear fruit in old age, they will stay fresh and green" (Ps. 92:12–14). And, man, I want that. Don't you?

Writing down your goals, like writing down your plan, is part of what God uses to cause this transformation. It's the water He uses to make good things happen. Leave a plant unwatered and untended, and you may not notice for a while that it's losing strength and health. Yet it's dying from the roots up. One day the lack of strength and health will start showing in the visible parts as well. But steady watering, day after day, can bring that plant back to flower if any life is left in it. It can still flourish, becoming fresh and green. No matter the lack of spiritual care you may have given your children—as I did for too many years—God can work through that water, poured out through His Word, to restore and renew and keep them growing for a long time. For a lifetime.

So start setting new goals for what you want to learn, apply, and accomplish as a family. One after another as your plan keeps coming together. Don't be concerned about starting small. In fact, be sure you *do* start small. Don't get carried away, over-watering the system and flooding it out, setting up everybody for frustration. Two or three goals a year is likely sufficient. Each of them very specific, attainable, and measurable, recognizable when you reach them and celebrated.

But more than anything, remember that the God who *gives* you the goals is committed and able to help you *accomplish* the goals. You're not competing with anybody. You're not padding your spiritual résumé. You're not acting as though you're somebody you're not. You're just raising the importance of your family's spiritual growth to the level of other areas of your life where you try to show steady progress and development. If goals contribute to bringing positive change *there*, why shouldn't they bring even greater change *here*?

CHAPTER 9

FUN FOR ALL AGES

*Step 5: Personalize Your Plan
to Fit All Your Children*

I'm so glad you have hung in there with me to reach this point of the book. I realize how daunting and overwhelming the process of vision-casting and goal development and some of these other kinds of advance work can potentially be in trying to shepherd your family with clearer purpose and direction. It's a big deal. It's not easy. And for most of us, it taps in to some spiritual muscles we haven't been quite as accustomed to exercising. So the fact that you are still here at this point makes you one of the exceptions to what I pray will increasingly become the rule for parents and grandparents who've been given the responsibility of raising the next generation of Christian disciples. I'm glad you're stirred with a renewed passion for that.

Let's take this opportunity to do a little bit of a reset, which I've found is often needed after thinking through some of the heavy topics we've been talking about in the last couple of chapters. If we're not careful and cognizant of the Enemy's schemes against us, he can twist around all of our good intentions until they seem like (a) too much work to do for somebody who already has way too much work to do, and/or (b) nothing more than the ingredients of another program, like the many failed programs we've already tried and that is sure to fail again.

This is not a program. It's not merely a schedule, not merely a syllabus. It's not a strict reordering of your family's weeknights. It's not a boring, awkward sit-down with mom and dad, one that's certain to incite resistance, if not outright rebellion, anything to avoid the discomfort of getting through it.

This is actually a new kind of lifestyle. It's as revitalizing and recharging on a Sunday morning or a Tuesday afternoon as it is on whatever other times of the week or month you might gather your family around the kitchen table to open the Word and see what spills out.

This process, which begins with a plan, is more of what you might call a paradigm shift. A home makeover. A comprehensive design intended to *enhance* your life, not further exhaust it—certainly not to handcuff you with assignments to meet and legalistic hoops to jump through. The results, equally as dramatic, have the potential to impact everything. Soon you'll start to notice you're growing closer together as a family; enjoying a freer, more natural form of intimacy and communication; making better, more prayerful decisions, large and small; inspiring one another to exciting new kinds of growth and opportunity; and watching your kids initiate changes that once required domineering supervision on your part (also known as *nagging*) while you become more effective at helping them integrate biblical truth and perspective more often into how they think and what they do.

It's amazing. It's God's work. It's simply how the Holy Spirit has promised to do His job whenever we put first things first and align ourselves in conjunction with His will and plan for our families.

In case you're wondering why I bring this up now, it's because I know what you may be thinking. I'm well aware of some of the excuses that can creep in and crop up at this stage of the game. And I know how many of those excuses can tend to congregate around one general area. It's this: you think the specific conditions in your home (whatever those conditions may be) make your particular family situation a no-go for this kind of plan.

You say your family dynamic is too disconnected or disinterested, perhaps even dysfunctional. Your kids: they're too spread apart in age. Your personality: it doesn't have the consistency or capability to give your spiritual authority any clout. Your life stage: everybody's too old now for this thing to work. It would've been great, you admit, regrettably, if you had come to this conclusion sooner, when your children were little.

No. Those are lies. And the joy of watching these lies fall to the power of God's transformative truth is something you do not want to miss experiencing. I guarantee you.

Here's what I want you to see, if you'll just give me another chapter, another chance to answer some of these brands of excuses. The rewards you're going to begin enjoying in your home will not become possible simply because you finally disciplined yourself boldly enough to pray and read the Bible together on a regular basis. That's a part of it, yes—a *big* part— but it's not the only part. The reason this plan can accommodate what everyone in your family needs is because now you're giving them *you*—your focus, your priority, your vision, your serious prayer attention—not just a fixed meeting time for doing a Bible thing. What you're really doing is turning tonight's devotional moments into tomorrow's teachable moments.

No one is too young or too old, no family too diverse, to learn memorable things about God and His ways when all of you are watching to see what He's going to show you next.

PLANNING FOR THE UNEXPECTED

I had taken my son along with me to buy a Christmas tree. We were a little late to be shopping for one that year for some reason, so the available inventory at the store was fairly picked over. I remember trying to locate the best-looking specimen I could find, tapping its base on the ground to be sure it could still hold on to all its needles and branches, when a teenage attendant appeared, asking if I'd found the one I wanted. I'm sure he could tell from the somewhat disappointed look on my face that I wasn't entirely pleased with my limited options.

"Look, I know we don't have a lot of good trees left. But if you'll just take this up to the cashier," he told me, fetching a pen from his pocket and writing out a number on what seemed to be an official-looking price tag, "you can have it for this"—about twenty dollars off what it was originally marked.

Great! I always like a good deal.

But as my son and I headed inside to pay, the thought struck me: *Wait a second. I wonder if that kid really has the authority to lower prices on merchandise.* I didn't want to get the boy in trouble or anything by ratting him out. Neither did I really want to pay full price for a Christmas tree that had probably been sitting there for three weeks.

But my son. What was I teaching my son? Was twenty dollars really worth the price of saying to him—with my actions (which are the very best teachers of all)—that you should always take what you can get? That you tell your conscience to quiet down and quit bothering you if it's about to cost you an advantage? That you play dumb if nobody is the wiser? And if you don't get caught, then you win?

I hadn't done anything wrong, obviously. And I certainly wasn't opposed either, had we been together in some other circumstance, to show my son the sound wisdom and stewardship of shrewdly negotiating for a fair price or outcome. But in this case, I was walking into the store, wrestling with a real, though perhaps fairly minor, ethical dilemma. I knew I could get the tree at a savings by handing the clerk the slip of paper I was carrying. But I might be letting a seventeen-year-old's lackadaisical, who-cares attitude toward his work and his employer determine the integrity of how I conducted business. What was I going to do?

Turns out, we bought the tree for the marked-down price, which was probably still more than it was worth. I checked with the cashier, and she assured me it was fine—that, yes, they were trying to clear out the trees. I would have paid the original price without a peep if the markdown had been incorrect. The fact that I got a bargain to go along with my little object lesson for my son, who saw his dad do the conscientious thing, was simply a nice bonus.

But I'd been tasked, not long before this moment arose, with coming up with a plan to lead my family spiritually—the kind of plan we've been talking about in this book. If all it entailed was an every-other-week devotional meeting and nothing transferred into real life on the *other* days of the week, my big plan wouldn't have been worth the paper it was written on. The plan leads to a promise. A promise to do and be for our kids what we need to do and be as their parents so our kids can learn to do and be what God is calling them to do and be as His children.

Now—full disclosure here—I shared this offhand story simply because it's the one that popped into my head as I was writing. I easily could've shared many more, however, where my example, instead, caused my spoken witness to take a real hit in the consistency department. I can think of far too many times when I've damaged the Lord's testimony in my life by the way I've acted, in the moment, in front of my wife and children. But when you're truly living by a plan, when your lives together are becoming more and more transparent, God can turn even your goofs and gaffes into teachable opportunities: opportunities for modeling repentance, opportunities for showing how to handle being disappointed with yourself so that a momentary failure doesn't turn into a long-term losing streak, and, most of all, opportunities for magnifying the grace and glory of God, who keeps loving us and restoring us even after we take a spill.

Those are the kinds of unplanned opportunities that arise only because you *do* have a plan. They won't arise—or at least you won't be likely to notice them—if you don't have a plan.

AGES AND STAGES

The different ages of your children will require different ways of thinking through the discipleship process because there are different ways of communicating and making connections with each of them. But rather than viewing this challenge as a problem, think of the privilege of continually looking for ways to make the attractiveness of life with Christ more real to them.

First, involve your whole family in creation of the plan. When everyone from your six year old to your sixteen year old is enthusiastically encouraged to weigh in on what you're trying to do, each child obtains their own measure of ownership in it. The more ownership they feel as part of what your entire family is trying to do, the more ownership they'll begin to develop for their personal, one-on-one relationship with Christ. While important for the success of the plan to involve each family member in the process, your role as the leader cannot be underestimated.

I've always felt—and the many success stories in business throughout history can attest to it—the leader must be the one who plants the vision. It's nice to imagine a grassroots vision and energy swelling up from underneath, strong enough to create and sustain lasting change. But leadership, though perhaps not always required in starting to *move* the needle, is certainly required in order to keep it pegged and pressing forward. This dynamic is as true for families like yours and mine as it is for churches and governments and multimillion-dollar corporations. So if you're the one in the position of spiritual authority in your home—father, mother, grandfather, grandmother, legal guardian, single mom or dad, whatever the case may be—ask God to give you a vision for your family, for your children. And faithfully keep that vision before them as the standard you're following, even on days when not everyone is feeling it quite so much.

Here's why I say that: *everything else* (besides the vision) is up for delegation. Everything else is ripe for opinion. By asking and expecting your kids to help you build out this plan, rather than forcing it on them from the top, it will be quicker for them to see how it can really help them with things they've sort of been wanting to do or wanting to learn but didn't exactly know how to go about it. Now they do. Now they can. Now they realize you're there, actively invested in coming alongside them to help them locate a path that gets them where they're hoping and needing to go. What's more, you, too, may be able to see—as opposed to what you've been fearing (the rolling eyes, the heavy groans, "I knew they were going to hate this")—an eagerness bordering on excitement coming back at you, enough to take all your fears away.

Give them the opportunity to dream with you. Give them the responsibility for taking charge of certain things. Give them the reinforcement of your full attention as they start asking the kinds of questions that used to rarely, if ever, come up before you began to deal more systematically and prayerfully with their issues. Let them play a big role in helping determine how this vision of yours takes shape in them in their own lives.

And second, help them develop specific goals for themselves. Your family, in order to stay united in purpose and in the Spirit, will always benefit from embracing certain spiritual goals in common. The things you do and pursue together will contribute to the shared identity that's so important to develop in your home. But your individual relationships with each child can really take a light-year leap forward as you help set personalized goals for their particular age or stage of spiritual maturity.

For the little ones, some of their goals may entail an expectation for answering two or three questions after the church service, such as (1) "What did the pastor talk about?" (2) "What did it mean to you?" (3) "How can you put that message into practice this week?" You can give them a particular chapter to read—Genesis 1, about creation; Psalm 1, about the blessings of obedience; the first part of John 1, about the nature of Jesus—and then plan a special time when you can sit down with them and talk about it. You might set a goal for them to learn the names of the books of the Bible, at whatever speed or pace you feel is realistic. It's completely up to your discretion.

Where will they learn these things if they don't learn them from you? Why should the church, or perhaps their Christian school, be primarily responsible for training them in what the Bible teaches? Why should they grow up struggling to know who God is, not sure where the great stories of Scripture are located, unfamiliar with their way around the one Book you say is the fount and foundation of all truth and instruction for their lives? If your kids aren't shown and shepherded at home how to understand Christ and apply His Word, seeing it modeled by the way you continue to pursue certain spiritual goals and desires, then who will show them?

I was sitting in a Bible study once, when one of the guys in attendance—a single man, young, maybe in his late twenties, early thirties—said something to the group like, "You know, I've always had to look outside of my family to try to understand faith. I mean, we went to church and stuff, but I don't remember my mother or father—either one—ever talking to me about Christ, ever reading the Bible with me, ever even helping me think through how to date a girl—even something as practical as that—in light of what God teaches and what was best for me. I'm left even now, as a grown man, just trying to figure it out on my own."

I sat there realizing as he was talking that the only reason we don't hear this kind of testimony more often is because people don't have places or occasions for saying it. I'm afraid this is the experience of many young men and women who grew up in so-called Christian homes—where Christ, for some odd reason, hardly ever came up in family conversations.

I'm not criticizing here. If I let it bother me, I could kick myself every day for all the opportunities I passed up, whole seasons of years when I never gave much more than a passing thought to helping my kids develop spiritually and fall more in love with Jesus. I may not know *all* the reasons why we parents shove this honor and responsibility down underneath our other goals and desires and reasons for living, but I promise you I'm personally acquainted with a whole lot of them. And I'm still trying not to be mad at myself about it—simply to receive God's forgiveness and do something about it.

But what if you set a goal for taking your children, at a particular stage of their spiritual development, through the entire book of Romans, showing them the whole grand sweep of God's salvation? What if you set a goal for taking them out, at a certain age of your choosing, to a cemetery one afternoon to show them the risk of taking drugs or abusing alcohol? What if you and your spouse actually set a goal for when either or both of you would initiate the first stages of a sex-talk with your kids, not simply giving them a description of the anatomical mechanics but offering a vivid explanation of God's purposes and why He's given us the freedom of sexual purity?

Think of the openness you'd be developing with one another if taboo topics weren't off the table but were part of how you intentionally interacted together. Think of the protection you could provide your children by enabling them to engage in important discussions within the safety of your home instead of within the cruel arena of the schoolyard or the confusing space of their own imaginations. Think of the trust you could earn (or rebuild) by letting them see your humble yet passionate desire to help them thrive spiritually, in ways you, perhaps, never knew until you were grown and making up for lost time.

The sky is the limit for goals you may want to set for your children. No one else knows your kids as well as you do. But you will come to know them even better as you guide them through some intentional age/stage goals to help them develop their growing faith. Best of all, they'll be coming to know God and His Word even better, putting them ahead of the game, spiritually, for kids their ages and putting them in a position to live out their faith in Him with deliberate devotion for a lifetime.

FROM HERE TO ANYWHERE

When I think back ten or fifteen years ago, when we first started having devotions together as a family, when we first started working structurally through specific goals we wanted each of our children to meet at certain ages and stages of their lives, I get a little choked up. I realize full well how depraved I am at heart, hopeless, if not for God's miraculous grace. I realize how underinformed and inadequate I was to teach them, especially as a younger dad, when I was still trying to grow in the Word and in prayer myself. I recall how basic some of our topics were even though, honestly, I was needing the refresher course as much as my kids, who may have been hearing it for the first time, at least from me.

This past year, during the regular intervals we enjoyed with our now-grown children, we studied *The Shorter Catechism*, a collection of systematic doctrine and practice that emerged from the fires of the Protestant Reformation in the 1600s. Incredible. (I didn't even know what a catechism was when we first started doing this years ago.) We had such deep, rich discussions on apologetics, grappling with huge questions, diving way down into the Word, and coming back to the surface with real treasures for the road.

Not only do I get to share with my kids what I've been learning in my own personal study, but they often are the ones leading our sessions now, leading out in prayer and leading my wife and me through the things God is showing them that I have never even thought of. They are sharing not only good Bible study material with us but also testimonies about some of the people they've been trying to lead to Christ, how they're ministering to one or more of their friends going through a hard time, stories about how God is opening doors for them to engage life-on-life with others, mentoring them, discipling them. I can hardly drink it all in. What God has done in our family—such an everyday, run-of-the-mill family—is enough to melt me away in overwhelmed gratitude.

I am reminded at times such as these that none of us—neither your family nor mine—is likely to experience these moments if not for building-block seasons when God was growing us slowly, helping our little five- and six- and seven-year-olds accomplish attainable goals that (as we strangely discover) are somehow harder to set than they are to reach. These are the small stepping-stones that lead to true spiritual adventure in the future, as well as to the joy, as Nehemiah 8:10 says, that grows up to become our strength. Not only *our* strength, but also our children's strength. What a blessing to watch. Truly, what a joy.

"Who dares despise the day of small things?" God asked through the prophet Zechariah (4:10). Not those whose vision for their family includes some *big* things that ride on the shoulders of God's *simple* things. As parents called to the spiritual leadership of our kids, we enjoy a front-row seat as God takes our faithfulness with a "few things" and multiplies them into "many things" (Matt. 25:23).

It's all so worth it. It's all so real. And when you look back at what will one day seem such a small, though important, investment of thought, prayer, and initiative—putting together your plan for making Christ known very specifically to each of your children—you will join me in letting out a deep sigh of worship for what He's done. Little things do add up. Little moments. Little experiences. And it doesn't take any bigger person than you (or me) to get it started.

CHAPTER 10

WHO DO YOU KNOW WHO NEEDS JESUS?

Step 6: Adopt a Family Prayer Focus

T he power and effectiveness of prayer is due in large part to the relationships it offers us. First, it allows us to have a relationship with God—worshiping Him, thanking Him, reaching out to Him as our loving Father—but also as a way for our relationship with Him to lead us by His Spirit into relationship with others. In essence, the work of prayer is the building of relationship.

That's why when we're praying with our kids—whether it's for one of their teachers who's been diagnosed with cancer, a problem one of them is having at school, or even one of those cute little prayers they sometimes pray about having a cut on their finger—the goal is not merely that God would intervene with help and healing, responding affirmatively to our faith and trust. The real beauty of prayer is that through this God-ordained go-between, He is enabling our relationship to be deepened not only with Him but also with one another. It's meant to enrich and intensify how we relate to our kids. How we relate to outsiders. How we open up and allow them to relate to us. Christ comes alive within these relationships, especially when they're connected by prayer.

Prayer unlocks things we may never know otherwise about one another; things that may not ever come up otherwise; wells of compassion we may not even feel, much less act upon; obsessions with self that could keep us from pausing long enough so we can truly empathize with another person. In prayer we're uniting under our shared relationship with Christ, asking Him—imploring Him—to move with might and glory to fix what's broken and supply what's missing. Despite how things may turn out, we still can be absolutely certain that by engaging in prayer, we already are receiving His blessing, simply by taking advantage of this divine instrument that entwines our hearts together: Getting to know Him. Getting to love Him. Getting to love what He loves—the people He has created in His image. Having the opportunity to know and be known by one another.

That's what I want my kids to experience when they practice and think of prayer. I don't want them seeing just a giant gumball machine—or perhaps one of those big mechanical claw machines near the entrance of the superstores. Put your fifty cents in, and you might win a prize. Or you might not. It's all up to how well you work the controls, how well you master the system and play the game.

Prayer is not a game. It's not a win-or-lose proposition. Prayer is always a win—a direct means of being in richer, fuller, deeper dimensions of relationship. If you and I, if my kids and your kids, if we all can learn *that*, that's what will keep us turning to God, turning to prayer throughout our lifetimes.

I realized, when I reached this point of developing our family's spiritual growth plan, prayer was going to be the thing that took it to the next level. Not just prayer, but prayer that led to action, prayer that led, through the Holy Spirit, into relationship. We could sit around learning Scripture all day every day. We could subsist on spiritual disciplines that are good at breaking down old patterns and building up new ones. We could even participate in prayer times for the general aches and pains of both the world and ourselves. But what we needed was a prayer *focus*. A focus outside ourselves. A focus that led to relationship. A focus on maybe just one individual, like, say, a family member.

Yes, of course. That was it! It tied everything together. Think back to step one, about recognizing God's role in our generational history, and step two, about sharing our personal testimony. Think about those middle steps about knowing our identity as a family, embracing our values and vision, then attaching meaningful goals that help put all these spiritual and eternal ideals into action. Everything comes together by funneling it into a prayer focus. Plus, above all, I could see how it tied into my larger passion—making Christ known for the purpose of enlarging and extending our family's legacy of faith into the future, down through the ages.

This was perfect. And prayer was how we'd do it. This plan of ours would never run the risk of becoming ingrown and overly introspective because it would always include a piece that sought out one external relationship, bringing this person's heart and soul and needs right where we could place them on our family altar and watch God make prayer work—in the way it was meant to work: by forging and strengthening relationships.

PRAYER HAS A NAME

The high spot for me in every workshop we lead is the moment when we get to this step. I ask people in the room—might be fifty, might be a hundred, might be a thousand, maybe more—to think of one person in their extended family whom they believe, from the best they can tell, does not have a relationship with Jesus Christ. I ask them to write down that person's name, to hold it before them as though they're placing it at the foot of the cross. And I say, "Would you join with me—everybody—in praying *out loud* for that one person while we all pray for ours?"

I wish you could hear it. I'm not sure there's another sound on the earth that is both as tender and as powerful as the sound of that audible prayer rising up from believing families. *Tender* because it's infused with a deep, holy compassion for someone who's more loved by a person and a family in that room than this individual probably knows. The years of spiritual longing and desire that are combined within that chorus of prayer outnumbers us all by decades, perhaps by centuries. But it's also profoundly *powerful* because if you take the few hundred people whose names are echoing forth from that gathering of parents and families, up through the rafters and into the heavens, you're talking about the makings of a harvest bigger than the size of most churches. Stretch it across a few years, and it's the size of a megachurch. You're positioning those prayers within the context of a dedicated plan that is going to see to it that these prayers keep happening—week after week, month after month, year after year. You're looking at the plausible likelihood that a whole bunch of the people whose names are on their lips that day are going to have the name of Jesus on their own lips before long.

The sound I hear in those prayers is the sound of a movement. An evangelistic movement. And it doesn't require going to Guatemala or standing on the street corner, or renting a stadium or canvassing door-to-door. All it requires is beginning to pray for someone you already know and love and watching where God chooses to take it.

And your kids get to see it all.

And be a part of it all. Firsthand.

Prayer is going to lead my family deeper into relationship with someone. People we care dearly about are going to know (in case they don't already know) how much we truly care about them. God is going to change some things through prayer, even if all He changes is us.

I'm good with that.

What I'm *not* good with—what I'm sorry that I was all too willing to be good with for way too long—is being satisfied knowing people only halfway, with too rarely stepping outside the cocoon of my own little world so I could better understand and walk with others in theirs—being content in assuming I was rich enough without being enriched by the stories and textures and fabrics that make up the larger portrait of my loved ones. I was so worked up over the cause of missions from my seat on the spiritual train that I zoomed past the people whose lives I could touch the most and who could touch mine the most.

I'm not saying the best part of this prayer journey hasn't been watching people open up to Christ in ways they'd sort of quit thinking about as their lives had gone on. That's enough to inspire some spontaneous worship like you wouldn't believe. I guess I'm just not sure God separates it out as distinctly as that. My family and I have been blessed by simply opening up new ways of spending time with certain family members, often in ways you may not classify as being spiritual in nature. When we decided at His direction to focus our prayers toward the lives of our extended family members, He was mainly calling us to love on them. And in the process of loving on them—and loving them enough to share Jesus with them—He's proven Himself capable of enlarging every aspect of our relationships with them.

So don't tell me this feels like lining up somebody in your sights and trying to notch their soul on your spiritual gun belt. What it feels like to me is lining up myself and my family in the center of God's will and letting Him guide us into investing ourselves, not in more playthings but in people.

And who's not good with *that*?

I've heard so many great stories from people who've embraced this step as part of their family plan. I hope some of the next stories I hear will be the ones coming from you.

PRAYER IN ACTION

As we began to pray about who we wanted to adopt as our family prayer focus for the first year—for a full year—the Lord brought to mind one of my uncles who lives in Chicago. His wife, my aunt, was a woman I knew to be a strong Christian and a faithful churchgoer. But my uncle, for reasons I guess I'd wondered about but never really asked, had never joined her in that. Great guy. Loved him to death. But to the best of my knowledge, he didn't have a saving faith in Jesus.

Since I was the one in our immediate family who had a relationship with him, I did what we've done with others in years since—just called him up, told him a little about what our family was doing, and asked simply, "Would you mind if we prayed for you throughout the coming year? We'd like to do that as a family—Wanda and the kids and I—if you're all right with it."

It didn't really matter if he was all right with it or not. We were going to be praying for him regardless. But we did want to give him the courtesy of knowing about it. While I'm sure asking someone this question might in some cases cause them to take offense or be cold and condescending in return—which could be your biggest worry right now when you consider the possibility—I can attest we've never yet asked this question of anybody who didn't say, "Yes, I'd love for you to do that. That means a lot to me."

But it's more than just praying for them. It's all about relation-ship, remember? The prayers that we launch from a distance, disconnected from knowledge of what's actually happening in a person's life, tend to have that feeling of being no more than wishes hard to believe in. But when you've committed, not only to pray for someone but also to spend some time with them and hang out together more, what you learn about what they need makes your prayers for them more intentional, more directly connected to who that person is and what he or she needs. Your prayers do not come from what you think he or she is likely struggling with or concerned about, but they are actually drawn from specific interactions with them, from looks on their faces, from admissions made from their own mouths.

This is real. This is real praying.

So I went to see him, my uncle, and had a great time catching up. After we made that commitment to pray for him, I learned stories about him, my dad, our family—even myself—that I had forgotten hearing, couldn't remember, or, in some cases, had no prior knowledge of. I'd honestly never heard some of this stuff. It was incredible.

We had so much fun. He loved being drawn out and thinking back. I couldn't get enough of it myself. And I told him, "We love you. You've always meant so much to me. And I want you to know that we're always here for you, that we want to be as big a part of your life as we can, and we want to help you in any possible way, including spiritually, because we're convinced that everything we need comes from Him, and we'd count it an honor to be praying with you about your needs, the same as we pray for ours."

He was really moved by that. I mean, how many people have ever said anything like that to you? I know you're a believer, so naturally you'd be inclined to appreciate this kind of gesture. But somewhere we Christians have picked up an avoidance complex, where in the interest of either keeping things comfortable or not risking rejection, we assume others consider our faith unwanted, uninteresting—that if we ever hope to influence them toward believing the gospel, we will need to try sliding it into their lives the way you hide medicine in the dog food and hope they don't see it coming. Maybe they'll swallow it down before they realize what they're chewing on. But the best way to give people the gospel is to give them yourselves. They may or may not receive it, of course. That's God's business, not yours. But they probably will receive you and your genuine love for them. And there's a whole lot of gospel flavor in that.

In the course of giving my uncle the gift of ourselves, our prayers, and our time—in giving him our family's relationship—we found he was actually eager to hear more, wanting to learn. So he and I started reading through the gospel of John together, meeting once a week by phone, just talking about what God was saying there, talking about who Jesus is and what His Word to us means. Our family was praying for him in the meantime, both together as a unit and individually, just bringing him and his needs before the throne on a regular basis. By the end of the fourth week, during one of our calls, he said to me, "Terence, I want Christ as my Lord and Savior. I don't know what all is involved in doing that, but I know I'm a sinner, and I know I need Him."

"You're sure?" I said.

"Yes, I'm sure."

I asked him if he'd get his wife on the phone while I called to Wanda to hop on with us too. Together we were able to hear my beloved uncle—my children's great-uncle—express his confession of faith in Christ, amazing us with the power of prayer and the power of what relationship with God can accomplish.

God even accomplished it ahead of plan (not *His* plan but *my* plan). We were a month into our yearlong goal and—check it out—we already had a new Christian in the family.

So I decided as part of our first year through this process, instead of moving on to the next person, we would continue pouring ourselves into my uncle's life. He and I kept studying the Bible together, working through four different books throughout the year. The kids would send him cards and little packages, would call him up sometimes to tell him they were thinking of him, praying for him. I can't remember when I'd had more fun, more incredibly satisfying fun. Our children, thanks to what God did, were getting to watch Christian faith break out in one of their family members with fresh excitement. And what's more, I knew prayer would forever have a hard time staying confined in their minds to just a little huddle of spiritual-sounding words—what nice Christian kids are supposed to do—all hopes and hot air, tacked on without much thought. God was building a relationship through it and building His relationship with them at the same time.

That's just the way He does it.

PRAYERFUL RESPONSES

Great things can happen in your home—and in your life—when you isolate your prayer in one focused direction, especially when you personalize it toward the needs of a family member.

First, you simply learn how to develop deeper relationships. I've mentioned this several times already, I know. But the importance of it goes beyond mere social skills. We live in a world where relationships are increasingly growing shallower and more artificial, heavy on perceptions and the making of impressions, measured in rising increments of "likes" and "followers." But the kinds of relationships that grow and develop through prayer put us in close enough proximity where we can really get to know someone. In order for our faith to speak to him or her with more than just chapter-and-verse conviction, we have to learn how to be transparent and vulnerable with the other person. He or she needs to see people humble enough to admit their own mistakes and to encounter people who are finding Christ sufficient for the specific needs and issues in their own lives. They need to be around a family who lets them all the way in, not one who turns into a different group of people when the porch light goes off for the night and the façades come in. Authenticity is not only in-dispensable in being an effective parent, a trust-building husband or wife, or a good friend—in any kind of relationship. It's also a key component of a truly effective prayer life.

Second, you grow more comfortable sharing your personal testimony. As I've said, your testimony is the most important story you can tell, and we tell it far too seldom. But the opportunity to intentionally pray and deepen your relationship with another person typically leads to another opportunity for sharing your testimony. We've actually set, as one of the age-stage milestones of our family, the goal of our kids' being able to share their personal testimony in three minutes or less, built again around that simple outline: life *before* Christ, how they *came to* Christ, and their life *after* Christ. Both we and our children need to be prepared to share this story easily, naturally, at the drop of a hat. And we can never get enough practice.

Third, it creates fresh material for teachable moments. One of the more noticeable but unplanned takeaways we've drawn from these types of experiences has been helping our kids learn a key character trait: trustworthiness. That's because the result of getting to know someone well can occasionally unearth some information that's not to be shared with just anybody. They'll feel free to share only as long as they're confident they can talk to you about things, knowing such personal matters won't go any further. Like you, we wanted our kids to learn how to minister effectively in up-close, life-on-life settings, how to be used by God to deeply impact their friends and others for Christ. And much of their effectiveness in doing this has depended on their being trustworthy, in being a discerning keeper of another person's heart. A life of prayer creates a world of moments that aid in the overall development of a believing, character-rich life.

And fourth, it helps reinforce your children's sense of identity. Your values, vision, and mission, as we've said, can help solidify your children's role within your family, helping them know what they stand for and what they're trying to accomplish in life. But the deliberate mission of keeping your children attached to extended family members—those who, until now, have perhaps put the "distant" in distant relatives—helps your kids see themselves within their larger family as well. As the generations grow farther and farther apart, separated by miles and isolated from shared experience, too many of us live as if we're on our own separate islands, adrift without attachment to the past and to one another. Every family, I realize, contains elements that are just easier to forget and ignore. But God has chosen to place us here on the earth within this distinct group of people. Not only does our hereditary access to them give us built-in avenues for loving them and caring for them in Jesus' name, but it also holds the potential to deepen our appreciation for where we've come from and how God has used our family history to help make us who we are.

I imagine, if you're anything like me, you've often realized you haven't even scratched the surface of prayer. You may sometimes even consider it more of a burden than a blessing, something you know you're obligated and expected to do but nothing that really feels all that essential and life-giving, more exercise than enjoyment.

What I've learned is that the problem is not so much a low level of desire or a lack of faith on our part, but simply that prayer doesn't work well in a vacuum. Prayer needs a focus. Prayers need direction and purpose. As long as we allow our praying to loop generically around the same old tired places and phrases, we can't expect to ever reach the point where we're actually meeting God through it, not just having another prayer meeting.

So I encourage you to affix a new focus to your praying, wherever you sense the Lord leading you to anchor it. But if you want a focus that I know from much experience will take your family on a true journey into how prayer really works, maybe you'd be interested in the one I've been describing. I have stood at the bedside of a dear family member, watching someone I love slip into eternity without ever receiving Christ as Savior, in spite of my best efforts to share about Him and describe Him. I concluded from that moment: never will another family member of mine leave this earth without at least *hearing* from me the truth of the gospel and the name of Jesus Christ.

I am passionately motivated by the vision He paints for us in Scripture, captured again within the teaching method of parable. In the midst of His stories about a lost sheep being found, about a lost coin being recovered, and about a prodigal son coming home, Jesus described the scene that takes place in heaven whenever a lost sinner is transferred by belief in the gospel from the kingdom of darkness and death to the kingdom of light and life. "I tell you," He said, there is "more rejoicing in heaven over one sinner who repents than over ninety-nine righteous persons who do not need to repent" (Luke 15:7). My uncle became cause for a party to break out in heaven. My uncle is going to be received with pomp and ceremony into God's eternal dwelling. Every time the Lord responds to the prayers of our individual families—of our spouses and our children—by claiming another believing soul from our network of relatives and in-laws and siblings and friends, we become part of a celebration that can't be contained to this world. Who couldn't get motivated to intercede for someone, realizing what God could be keeping in store for them by working through the love we already have for them?

That'll put some focus behind your praying. And that'll lead your family into an experience in which prayer becomes what prayer was intended to be. God may or may not handle those prayers exactly the way you're asking. But you watch—He *will* use the situation to foster and deepen relationships. Praying *with* someone, praying *for* someone is always an opening for greater relationship—if not directly with that person, then certainly with the God who's still reaching for that person.

When we know what prayer is meant to do, when we know what it's been given to us for—when we know how prayer really *works*—every one of our relationships will begin to intersect with it and be impacted by it. Then prayer will no longer be a chore or a challenge, either for ourselves or our children. It'll be how God directs us with bold sensitivity into others' lives.

Make sure prayer is not just a ribbon and a bow on your plan. Make it an active, integral part of your plan.

CHAPTER 11

LIVE IT LIKE YOU MEAN IT

Step 7: Draft Your Family Covenant

As we reached the end of our time together at the lake—
that first little retreat I told you about, where Wanda,
the kids, and I discussed embarking on a new spiritual plan for
our family—we still didn't know exactly what we were doing
or where we were going with it. Those blank lines on our Blue
Sheets were still waiting for answers. But we knew we'd struck
a chord. Each of us was in total, enthusiastic agreement that we
wanted to press forward into this new direction at full speed.
We wanted to learn more about Christ and His Word; wanted
to develop a stronger defense for our faith; wanted to experience
an active, coordinated mission that carried out what God had
already begun within our family and what we prayed He would
keep on growing within us by His grace.

We wanted it all. For all the right reasons. And I know you
want it too.

I share with you a sense of excitement, thinking about how
God's Spirit can bring you closer together as a family, how an

intentional plan can both simplify and electrify everything that happens in your house. Instead of simply assuming, unspoken, that everyone generally thinks of Christ as being at the center of your home, you can be confident now that you're keeping the path clear for Him to move freely, without restraint, in each of your lives. Submission to His total lordship and His direction in your family can become your deliberate aim, a living reality. The noticeable changes, opportunities, contentment, and tones of voice that can now work themselves more consistently to the surface will bring a refreshment to your spirit that perhaps you haven't experienced in a long, long time. That would be wonderful.

Much of what I remember about that cabin weekend was how I felt seeing our kids light up at the possibilities, noticing how they were catching the vision for what God had birthed in us as parents. But one part of the plan I hadn't really contemplated before that moment, which has come to be a significant aspect of how our family now operates, is the idea of a *covenant*—making promises to one another to help secure the future we envisioned.

I don't recall who said it first—may have been me, my wife, or even one of the children. But the idea bubbled up from somewhere that if we were truly serious about charting a new course for our family, we needed to agree on some commitments that would guard against any slippage in conviction. If goals are like milestones that help you know you're moving down the right road, covenant is what helps you make sure the car keeps rolling. Past *every* milestone. Now and forever. So we made some covenants that day, and we're still keeping them.

One was the covenant that we would stay committed to this plan for the rest of our lives. We weren't going to graduate anybody out of class when they reached a certain age. Wouldn't be handing them their diploma in applied discipleship and then sending them off into the world. We promised to keep our every-other-week family devotional as a standing appointment, even after the children grew up and left the house. This was to be our gathering point, our meeting place, for life.

We also committed that as the years went on, and as God gravitated the kids toward a person whom they were beginning to think of as their "significant other"—one who might potentially become that child's husband or wife—they would not agree to marriage until that individual had become a part of our family's devotional experiences. Any movement toward engagement and wedding plans would come with the corresponding understanding that we'd be adding another seat in the basement on Sunday nights (or another extension on the conference call) so we could enjoy becoming acquainted not only with the person's face around the house but also with his or her life and spiritual heartbeat.

Doesn't that sound like a reasonable request? God's Word, as I've mentioned before, is clear that as believers, we're told to keep ourselves out of significant relationships in which we are unequally "yoked" with unbelievers. So if someone were to duck away from making a marriage commitment to one of our children because he or she didn't want to relate to the rest of us on a spiritual basis, I'd call that a well-placed red flag, wouldn't you? That's the kind of early warning sign that can spare a young Christian man or woman from borrowing a lifetime's worth of trouble, from foolishly considering a fiancé's lack of faith to be a little something that can be adjusted and corrected in due time once that ring is on his or her finger.

We've had the pleasure of spending a year or more of high-quality time with each of the people who are now our son-in-law and our daughter-in-law. We've benefited from their relationships with Christ while being able to feed into theirs from ours. Plus, we've provided our children a safe, secure, established means of interacting with their spouse-to-be in ways that might never have taken place if not for a covenant made when they were kids.

I love that.

Now, promises are easy to break, of course, even when made with the best of intentions. But something tells me these promises of yours, as those of ours, will become special ways of adding layers of togetherness to your ongoing experiences at home. The distinctive of a covenant, when kept, is that it will always result in blessing. And the covenants you make and keep as a family will result in blessings that last beyond your lifetime.

WHAT COVENANT MEANS

The story of the Bible is the story of covenant. Even the way the text is organized—into Old and New Testaments—confirms the centrality of this message because the word *testament* could just as easily be translated as *covenant*. While some of the various covenants in Scripture contain elements that are more indicative of a *contract*, where certain conditions must be met or else the promise can legally be rescinded, the covenants made by God to man are unconditional. Sure, they expect a certain response. They reward obedience and deal appropriately with lack of compliance. But they are binding agreements. Made by almighty

God. And, ultimately, they are dependent on His faithfulness alone.

The writer of Hebrews said, "When God made his promise to Abraham, since there was no one greater for him to swear by, he swore by himself, saying, 'I will surely bless you and give you many descendants'" (6:13–14). There was simply no further discussion or paperwork needed. There was absolutely no doubt about it. God was going to do what He said He would do. That's why, as the passage goes on to say, Abraham did nothing other than to wait patiently—or what some would call *not* so patiently—after which he "received what was promised" (v. 15).

As God said.

So as you read the grand sweep of the Bible—God's covenants with Adam, with Noah, with Abraham, with Moses, with David—you keep seeing this theme emerge. His people forget what He's done for them. His people are contentious and inconsistent. His people sometimes even stumble into outright rebellion, idolatry, and apostasy. Yet He keeps reaching out and redeeming a remnant. He never stops seeking His people. He always remains faithful to His covenant.

God's covenant of grace appears as early as Genesis 3, when Adam and Eve, trying to grapple with their sudden plunge from perfect innocence into paralyzing guilt, hear God curse the serpent (meaning Satan) and make a promise concerning the woman's offspring (meaning Jesus), that He will one day "crush" the serpent's head (v. 15). Now, Adam and Eve, obviously, had failed to steer clear of sin. They had eaten from "the tree of the knowledge of good and evil" despite being told in the most direct of terms, "When you eat from it you will certainly die" (Gen. 2:17). Yet God had already made plans for this occurrence, to extend grace not only to them but also to those of us who would come from them. As Paul would later write, "Grace was given us in Christ Jesus before the beginning of time" (2 Tim. 1:9). *Before the beginning of time.* That means even when the first man and woman were swallowing down their death sentence, God's covenant was already at work to seek and save His people from among fallen humanity.

That's His covenant to us. That's His binding promise. "Lord, you have been our dwelling place / throughout all generations. / Before the mountains were born / or you brought forth the whole world, / from everlasting to everlasting you are God" (Ps. 90:1–2). He provides for those who are called by His name, and "he remembers his covenant forever" (Ps. 111:5).

Over and over again, throughout the pages of the Old Testament, God's people—Israel—cycled between awed obedience and dismissive arrogance, between good and evil. God worked to get their attention by allowing other nations to dominate and oppress them, which typically resulted in Israel crying out to Him for help and deliverance, in making new promises of loyalty and worship. But since they persisted in failing to keep their promises and, therefore, live within His promises of abundance and blessing, He finally sent the great empires of the day (first Assyria, then Babylon) to conquer them and take them captive. Yet as stories such as those of Ezra and Nehemiah confirm—in which the Jews returned home from exile to rebuild Jerusalem and to renew their devotion to the law—we see God working to restore and reestablish them. Despite the insult of their ingratitude and apathy, despite their historical patterns of sin, "he was merciful; / he forgave their iniquities / and did not destroy them. / Time after time he restrained his anger / and did not stir up his full wrath. / He remembered that they were but flesh, / a passing breeze that does not return" (Ps. 78:38–39).

The refrain repeats itself again and again—in places as far-flung as the books of Exodus, Numbers, Nehemiah, Jonah, and Joel, as well as in the writings of King David: "The LORD is compassionate and gracious, / slow to anger, abounding in love" (Ps. 103:8). We can count on His "love in the morning" and His "faithfulness at night" (Ps. 92:2)—every day, every night, all day, all night—because He always keeps His promises to His people.

He is a *covenant-keeping God.*

YOU, TOO, CAN BE A COVENANT KEEPER

I realize that not every family, even after the dedicated work of putting a plan in place, is certain of gaining acceptance of it from every child. I'm aware that those who hope this idea will repair all the brokenness and struggles and problem areas in their home can't be completely assured of seeing immediate, measurable results. I know of grandmas and granddads who want to put a book like this one into the hands of their grown children, praying it will steer them to lead their own families in the ways of the Lord as they were taught at home. Truth is, the promises made by any of our children to stay true to these values and this vision and their relationship with Christ are not guaranteed to be maintained into adolescence and adulthood.

But you and I as parents must look to God as our model. For we know well how much trouble we ourselves have caused Him as *His* children. We don't really need to scour the pages of

Scripture to tut-tut the children of Israel for not recognizing the kind of life God was offering them if they would simply obey. We know better than to blame them. We've been in those shoes more times than we can count. Even though God, in His patient perseverance, has chosen to graft the Gentiles into the vine of His covenant promises, extending the gift of salvation to all who believe (Rom. 1:16), we many times have been reluctant followers. We have stood here as the recipients of more grace and more rescues than anyone in our position should ever hope to be given, yet we have often turned away at the next opportunity, when God didn't arrange the circumstances to suit us.

We know what it means to break a promise. We've broken quite a few of them. But God has been faithful, hasn't He? Faithful to discipline, yes, but faithful also to forgive and redeem on the other side. He's been faithful to keep His promises to wayward, forgetful children, like us, who are so predictable sometimes at not keeping ours.

I know, especially when your children leave home and assume the management of their own lives and lifestyles, you can't always control how they choose to respond to you or how diligently they dedicate themselves to staying grounded and growing in faith. But you can keep your covenant to *them*. You can maintain prayer for *them*. You can stay surrendered, sacrificial, dependent, and humble in your heart for *them*—leading and loving by example—so they can see in you the unconditional covenant nature of God that can help draw them back to their spiritual senses, just as His covenant has so often drawn us back to ours.

Covenant is key to what is meant by leading our families spiritually. You and I do not enter into this process lightly, nor do we intend to stop fulfilling our commitments to it at any point in the future. There is nothing too hard—for you or for me—that should make us shy away from stepping into this role, from embracing this calling from God. And we do it with the full awareness that we are doing it for keeps. We are making this our promise. We are not letting go of what God has gripped our hearts to pursue. We are planting our feet at this juncture in the stream of generational history where He has positioned us.

And we are declaring it our legacy.

FROM NOW ON

Those two covenants our family made—to continue implementing this plan throughout our lifetimes and to incorporate any significant others into our family devotionals as a condition for marriage—have continued to prove enormous blessings in our lives, fanning out across the years from that little lakeside cabin so many years ago.

But maybe my favorite of all is a third covenant that completely sealed the vision God had birthed within me, the vision for which Wanda's question had been the catalyst and that had now progressed into the creation of our Generational Spiritual Development Plan. As we kept talking about our covenant, the kids did more than simply promise to stick spiritually with their mom and me and their siblings for the remainder of their lives, experiencing growth and discipleship with the ones they loved in their family of origin. They also made a covenant with us that they would introduce and implement this plan with their own families, as God gave them children of their own to raise in the nurture and instruction of the Lord.

I knew then, from the way their statement struck me, that God had really been changing my heart in the months and years leading up to that moment. I'm sure there had been times in my life, even as a husband, even as a parent, when a statement like the one they were making would have left me feeling . . . oh, happy? Impressed? Glad to hear it? But in light of what God had been teaching me throughout the process of developing my own life plan, taking me to the altar where He'd been showing me through His Word and through prayer what He wanted me to be as a husband and a father—as a man—no remark or revelation could possibly have filled me with more joy. The thought of my kids sitting around the table with *their* kids, teaching and training them how to sit around the table with *their* kids—my great-grandkids—learning and living the ways of the Lord . . . I thought I'd died and gone to heaven. I knew that's what I'd been placed on this earth for. That's what I'd been praying for as I contemplated how to put into practice my "one thing" of making Christ known to my kids. I realized, of course, this plan we were putting together was something they needed, a deliberate way of helping them grow up as young people in the faith. But as much as they needed it, I needed it, too, especially that evening. I needed to hear what was being discussed and tossed around as precious promises between these precious members of my family.

My wife and I weren't just trying to get them ready for college anymore. God was throwing open the door to get *all* of us ready for whatever He wanted to do with us then and for the rest of our lives.

CHAPTER 12

MOMENTUM-
BUILDING MOMENTS

An eight-year-old girl was having some outdoor pictures made among the fall colors in a Nashville park one Sunday afternoon, when a lone jogger emerged from one of the running trails that snaked alongside. The runner, a young woman dressed in navy blue sweats and a zip-up jacket, slowed to a gentle stop, fumbled her earbuds loose, leaving them to dangle from around her neck and shoulders, and just kind of stood there. Watching. The photographer, becoming aware of the woman's presence, looked up from her camera for a moment, long enough to give a quick glance of polite but dismissive acknowledgment. *We're working here.*

Then suddenly, stunned recognition passed across the photographer's face, as well as the faces of the little girl's parents and family members who were standing nearby. Noticing how their stares, their mouths all slightly agape, were now focused on something behind her, the little girl, too, turned to see what was causing the interruption.

Now *she* began staring as well. Breathing harder. Speechless. This obviously wasn't just some casual weekend runner bouncing along.

It was pop music star Taylor Swift.

Seeing everyone sufficiently flatfooted, the young singer smiled and skipped down the uneven stone stairs into the grass, approaching the little girl. "Hi. Okay if I get my picture made with you?"

No words from the little girl. Just a broad smile and nervous, exaggerated nodding.

The photographer instantly started snapping extra frames, hurrying to capture the moment while the multi-award–winning singer/songwriter—whose face and image appear regularly, almost daily, on glossy magazine covers and other media spaces the world over—hung around for a while to see if she could help out with the girl's photo shoot.

"Try this. Now stand this way. No, more like this," she'd say, striking the desired pose and facial expression for the girl to copy. They laughed, chitchatted, everybody soaking up their surprise brush with celebrity on an otherwise ordinary day. Then, with a wave and a quick good-bye, the "Shake It Off" singer was dashing off for the rest of her run while the young girl and her parents looked around at one another—smiling, then squealing, their heartbeats slowly beginning to regulate.

"You *do* know who that was, don't you?" the photographer asked her.

Again, no words. Just both-hands-over-her-mouth amazement.[1]

---

1 Jordan Buie, "Taylor Swift surprises Fans, Photobombs Nashville Park Portraits," *Tennessean*, November 13, 2014, www.tennessean.com/story/news/local/2014/11/08 /taylor-swift-surprises-fans-photobombs-park-portraits/18718813.

Oh my goodness. That was Taylor Swift.

If I were guessing, I'd say this little eight-year-old girl had probably already been a Taylor Swift fan. If not a big fan, she at least was well aware of her and knew a sizable number of interesting facts about her. She'd read things about her. She'd heard things about her. And even if she hadn't been in the habit of buying Taylor Swift albums up to that point in her life—in whatever way kids "buy music" anymore—I'm guessing that she has probably bought every song of hers ever since. This little girl now is, as they say, "bought in."

That's what we all want to happen with our children as we seek to introduce them more intimately to the One whose words and ways are substantially more valuable than those of any pop star or movie star or sports star or any other star enjoying their moment in the sun within today's cultural galaxy.

We want our kids to know Jesus Christ.

- Who is He?
- Is He real?
- Why did He come to earth?
- What has He done for us?
- Why do we need Him so much?
- Is He really who He claims to be?

And if He truly is who He claims to be, wouldn't we be foolish not to want to investigate Him, to learn everything we can possibly learn about Him, to listen again and again to what He has to say until His Word becomes second nature to us, in our minds, on our lips, until we're humming those words not only through the house but also repeatedly throughout the day? Wouldn't we want to be followers of Someone who can do what He does, who's done what He's done, and who will continually do things in our lives that we can worship Him and thank Him for, now and throughout all eternity?

This leads me to say again: This *plan* we've been discussing and desiring is not just a plan. This *process* we've been learning is not just a process. This is a sea-change opportunity for us to lead our families—in whatever way His Spirit leads us—so that we and our children can come to know Jesus Christ in the most personal, all-the-time, as-you-go, totally immersed way possible.

And while part of this plan and process, by its nature, will always feature some kind of ongoing, set-aside moments of prayer, Bible study, worship, and spiritual dialogue, we should never underestimate the power of strategic, creative, momentum-building moments, when we're able to make this relationship with Him come fully alive. For the whole family.

From the establishment of new traditions, to the scrapping of unnecessary old ones, to the making of fresh memories, to the exciting opportunities when our families can serve others together, we are perfectly positioned as parents to enhance in our kids what knowing Christ can really mean.

Hey, Taylor Swift may be a big star. Good for her. How nice of her to pop in on a little girl like that unawares, completely making a whole family's day. But Jesus not only created all the Taylor Swifts of the world, He also created . . . uh, the world. And the sun. And the stars.

What kid shouldn't love meeting *Him*?

WHY WE DO WHAT WE DO

When I think of the special moments that mean the most to the Chatmon household, my mind immediately runs to Christmas dinner. Mmm, I could get hungry just sitting here thinking about it. Wanda does it up right. I'm talking hot entrées, all the side dishes, and desserts, served buffet-style in a long row of chafing trays. There's nothing skimpy about what's there for us to fill up our plates. But while I do love every last bite, and make sure I always get my seconds before I'm through, the part that makes our Christmas dinner special is what happens around all the food and the fixings.

First, all my kids and their families are going to be there. At least they've never missed one yet. They know, even as adults, their mom and dad want them to protect this particular once-a-year engagement on their calendar.

Second, we'll usually be joined by twenty or thirty others—extended family members who've been able to come, as well as other friends we've invited who perhaps don't have family in the area. Some of these same friends have been coming to Christmas dinner for ten, fifteen years or more. We've watched their kids grow up from toddlers to teenagers during that time, season after season. They're as much a part of the celebration as are our own kids. Together with the occasional uncle or aunt or grandparent or cousin or whoever, all these extra settings around the table represent part of the high value we place on family legacy and extravagant generosity.

One of my nephews, for example, was in attendance from California at one of our gatherings. He was the family member we'd adopted as our prayer focus for that year, and we'd been thoroughly enjoying getting to know him better in the months leading up to it. He was looking for work at the time, as I recall, so we invited him to come visit us, bought him a plane ticket, and were so blessed by his presence, by the chance for all of our kids to love on this family member they'd been praying for and caring for all year long.

"Why would you do this for me?" he asked when I told him we were expecting him, that he was welcome to come. It was just another living example of our family values and our family mission, right there around our table. The building of relationship. Another brick in the building of our faith. Fresh building material for our worship.

I'm sure you're picking up on the idea that I put some thought and emphasis behind our annual Christmas dinner. I consider it rather sacred. Everyone who's there, before they dig in, knows there's a ritual to this process. I'll be standing up to share a few words about what God has been doing in our family throughout the year, how He's been working with us, and what He's been teaching us—all reasons to praise Him and be thankful. Oh, maybe it'd be a little inaccurate to call the length of my talk a "few words." My wife and kids would probably say it's *a lot* of words. While I always ask if others would be interested in sharing as well, they usually—by the time I've said my *few* words—keep *their* words to a more appropriate length.

But it's a *moment*, a momentum-building moment. A moment when we realize and reaffirm that we're not just here because it's Christmas. We're here because we're Christians. We're here because God, in His totally illogical grace, humbled Himself, came to earth, and chose by His own wise, inscrutable providence to establish us through faith as His beloved children. So, honestly, *we shouldn't be here.* We should, instead, be punished beyond the point of death for our sins, our rebellion, and our rejection of His kindness. Yet He provides us the privilege of celebrating with one another the greatest gift of all—not only baby Jesus in a manger but also King Jesus in our hearts.

I don't know what kind of traditions your family enjoys or whether you're, perhaps, the kind of person or family who doesn't particularly go in for much ceremony and seasonal markers. That's fine. But some of what's available to us as parents that we can transform for truly Christ-centered purposes are the standard traditions that populate our typical calendar year.

Use your imagination. I'm thinking of birthday celebrations, for example. I know there's usually cake and candles and presents, maybe a few friends and a party. But how might you reinvent the way birthdays are marked at your house, based on some of the values that shape you as a family?

I'm thinking of summer vacation. What with the sagging economy and some of the shifts toward non-regular work hours and 24/7 connectivity, I realize the time-honored summer vacation is sadly becoming a thing of the past. But what if you not only reinserted it into your family's set of traditions but also reinvented it by planning it with some of your spiritual goals in mind?

I'm thinking of pizza and movie night. Perhaps your family does something along these lines as part of your weekly or almost weekly routine. That's great, of course, and don't hear me suggesting that you turn it into a prepared Bible study instead. But again, use your imagination. Pray about it. Brainstorm about it. The Lord might turn this informal tradition of yours on its head in some way that creates a regular opportunity for you to reinforce what He's doing with you spiritually as a family.

Every moment can be a God moment.

Even though I've told you what I love so much about our Christmas dinner, I haven't actually told you the best part yet. Once dinner is over, once everybody, except our children and their mates, has cleared out, that's when we all get comfortable, down in the basement, to talk and laugh and reminisce a little. And that's where we conduct our annual planning session for what we want our next year of family devotionals and family goals to comprise.

We'll debrief on what we liked or didn't like about how things went the previous year. We'll share with one another about what's most on our hearts and what we'd love to consider studying or doing in the year ahead. We already know whether we're coming up on a Connection year, a Commitment year, or a Commission year (the three-year cycle we use for our particular plan). So we'll each have been thinking in terms of what this might look like for our family.

The role I assume as the spiritual leader is to gather up all the discussion that takes place around this cozy Christmas hangout and then throughout the next week create a Bible study plan for us to try following for the balance of the new year. It's a fantastic time and a fantastic way to be together. God has led us to capitalize on a time that could just as easily become lost to shopping and football and people rushing off to catch up with their other friends who are in town. But we've said, "You know what? We're making this our tradition. I'm not putting my *foot* down, but we are putting our *faith* down because honoring this tradition and doing it this way can truly keep changing our lives forever."

I think you might love making plans for that.

FAMILY IN ACTION

If I could want anything more fervently than what God has been motivating me toward desiring for the past ten or fifteen years—wanting my kids to know Christ in ever-increasing ways—it would be this: wanting my kids to help others know Christ. The thought of God using my children to share His love and to help disciple other people in the Word is . . . man, it just thrills me to the bone. That's a true momentum motivator for me.

When you've been helping your kids systematically learn about Jesus—who He is, who they are, what truth is, the kinds of things that can start to become regular conversation material around your house—He can turn those kids of yours into little dynamos of ministry, even at an early age. They don't need to wait until they are eighteen or in college before they are ready to talk about Christ with their friends or reach out to the lost and least around them. Sure, you want them to grow spiritually, but some of the most incredible instigators of growth are those hands-on opportunities they experience as children, where they're serving and sharing and watching their faith multiply before their very eyes. So always be looking for ways to foster this kind of heart and attitude within them—again, I say, from an early age—helping them work alongside you, seeing their parents devoted to giving and serving, to leading and mentoring and discipling.

If you're not sure where to start, just start with your church. Plug in to a ministry through which, perhaps, your whole family, kids and all, can become involved. Our church, in cooperation with dozens of other churches in the greater Atlanta area, participates in a huge ministry initiative called Unite!—where hundreds and hundreds of volunteers can step into the waters of Christian service. Our family has joined in several times by helping put together care packages for the homeless—blankets and Bibles and food and everything—that we then help distribute. The churches also conduct a big weekend in the inner city every fall, complete with a picnic and lots of donated giveaways for the poor and needy. We've participated in that event as a family, meeting other families, tossing a football, but also sharing our story and the gospel. These kinds of opportunities abound when you're really looking for them.

As I mentioned earlier, taking a whole-family mission trip is another great idea. Churches and ministry organizations are increasingly seeking participants for short-term mission projects—as you've likely seen and heard about—not simply going from village to village to share about Christ and how to be saved but also doing construction projects and providing other needed services that contribute to an area's well-being. How many times have you heard men and women come back from one of these trips telling how it completely changed their lives, how it blew up their inward-minded perspectives, how transformative it was in helping them become more sacrificial toward others in Jesus' name, more confident in sharing their faith? But what if, instead of a dad or mom or a big brother or big sister coming home, showing around their pictures to everybody, trying to convey in words what the experience was like, what if *everybody* had been there to actually experience it for themselves, together? Think what a milestone and memory it would create for your entire family to keep recalling and building on.

Pray about that.

But any of these suggestions—from local ministry projects to overseas mission trips—would most likely be once-a-month, once-a-year, once-in-a-lifetime types of experiences, which are great. But the part of life that's much more daily, the part that gives each of us—ourselves and our children—the opportunity to make the greatest, deepest impression on others' lives is our regular, ongoing interaction with friends, coworkers, neighbors, and other acquaintances. And their families.

My prayer for this book is that God would use it to help you make Christ known to your children and throughout your family. My bonus prayer for this book is that God would use it to help *us*—all of us—minister Christ and make Him known to other families. The joy of watching Him work inside our homes and helping to unite us in Him is an incredible thing, but watching Him take what He's growing here and then transplant it into other people's lives is a big part of what is meant by Jesus' commission to go into all the world and "make disciples" (Matt. 28:19)—not just into *the* world but into *your* world, into *my* world, into our *kids'* world.

Family-on-family discipleship. That is my dream.

And we've seen it come to life, in simple but significant ways, as God's Spirit works within our existing relationships, giving us opportunities to share who He is and what He's doing. Many times one of our children has been talking with one of their friends, who'll begin to open up about problems he or she is experiencing at home or maybe personally. Or perhaps their friends will express—even if they're part of a Christian family—how they wish they could talk with their parents about the kinds of things that we, in our home, now routinely discuss and pray about together. Wanda and I—same thing. It just comes up. People will ask, "How do you do that? How do you get your kids interested in the Word?"

"Well, let's get together sometime, and we'll talk about it."

This has led to so many chances for us to share with and encourage people. To bring some of our kids' friends into our home, not just for the free hot dogs and soft drinks but for good times of learning and listening, of sitting around talking and opening God's Word with them.

I'm afraid that when our ministry and service toward others is not housed and flowing through what God is already doing with us as a family, then we end up, ironically, being fragmented by our faith instead of united by it: Dad's off tonight and tomorrow night for a meeting at church. Mom's off at her women's Bible study. The kids are off with their youth group at camp or on a weekend retreat. There is nothing wrong with any of that—it very well could be exactly what some of us need to be doing on any given day or week. But it just might also be activity for activity's sake. While it may feel good and seem important at the time—and it may actually even *be* important—whenever our expression of Christianity isn't regularly feeding back into our family and then being directed by God's Spirit back *through* our family, I'm just telling you, it can sometimes sap the spiritual life out of you, instead of becoming part of how God helps your kids know and love and experience Him. If we miss out on that, I'm not sure what we've accomplished of any great value.

I'd love to think of your home becoming a place where personal discipleship happens. I'd love to think of your kids' friends and their parents enjoying a cookout on your back deck, then going inside together for an hour or so, praying for one another and promising to get together again soon to talk about what God has been doing in the meantime. And, perhaps most of all, I'd love to think of children who've been brought up in this kind of environment—where family-on-family discipleship is simply the understood expectation of what families do—growing up to raise families of their own who can start right away, as young couples, already looking for people to mentor and walk alongside. Wouldn't that be beautiful? And every new experience would be building momentum for the next one.

This is not the work of the preacher's family; this is the work of *your* family and *my* family. It's a privilege. It's an honor.

Remember, I'm no Bible scholar. You're probably not either. I have a business degree from the University of Illinois. I'm trained to spot talent and manage workflow and analyze budgets and recognize a good marketing strategy when I see it. But here's the chance for people like us to take a wide-angle view at how we're doing life, to see where we are, perhaps, just bobbing along without really even thinking about how our faith and values can affect so much more than just which lot we park our car in on Sunday mornings.

The only thing God is looking for when He looks to you as the leader of your home is *you*. When you start seeing this plan of yours as a whole-life plan, that's when He can turn your prayerful imagination loose to infuse all kinds of family moments with fresh breezes of purpose, churning up the kind of momentum that can change everyone's life for good.

PART III

THE PURSUIT

CHAPTER 13

SUFFICIENT TO
THE STRUGGLE

If I could leave you with only one word, after sharing so many with you already, I'm not sure what that one word would be. If you'd be willing to allow me *two* words, I'll settle on two that could be the best way for us to wrap up our time together, one for this chapter and one for the last. Those two words are *sufficiency* and *legacy*.

We began this book by looking at the calling involved in leading our families spiritually. A serious calling. A holy calling. One of the things I know about it—based not only on my own experience but also on the repeated experiences of others—is how this calling intrinsically resonates within the hearts of believing parents. I don't think I'd be exaggerating, not by even a single notch on the yardstick, to say we *all* want to rise up to the full stature of this God-ordained directive in our lives. It pulses within our core the way few other things can.

I don't doubt for a minute that your hunger and desire for seeing your children come to faith and truly embrace Him as their reason for living is totally genuine, soul-deep, anchored in the bedrock. I never feel the need to try convincing anyone of the *what* and the *why* behind this sense of purpose we all feel. The hesitations don't begin to appear until we start progressing toward the *how*. If we're going to get hung up, that's typically the place where it happens. *We simply don't know how to do it.* But some of the answer has, I hope, started to become clearer as you've been thinking through the various components we've been imagining in this book, the idea starters that could perhaps become part of your own family plan for spiritual growth. Or maybe you've received a good part of the answer simply by recognizing your *need* for a plan. That's actually a big step right there, all by itself. Many parents will say, "Yeah, I think I kind of know what I need to do. I just haven't written it down."

Well, no. I'd say the reason they haven't written it down is that they *don't* know what to do.

I know. I've been there.

Either way, we come back around to the same place. The *how* is what keeps this towering hurdle stuck between our wants and our reality. While the development of a solid plan is certainly part of the answer—part of what brings this hurdle down to size—the ultimate one-word answer to every *how* question is *sufficiency.*

Christ our Lord is sufficient to this task.

An illustration from Jesus' life, found in Matthew 17, may help to explain. After the mountaintop experience, where His inner group of disciples had seen Him transfigured in dazzling glory—standing between Moses and Elijah, with the voice of God Himself booming around them—they came down the hill to find a waiting crowd, as usual, eager to ask something of the

Healer and Teacher. One man in particular ran up to Him, say-ing, "Lord, have mercy on my son" (v. 15). The boy had long been suffering from seizures, his father said, which made life nearly unbearable, putting his son in constant danger of causing him-self fatal harm. "I brought him to your disciples, but they could not heal him" (v. 16).

Jesus' response to this situation indicates a measure of agita-tion. You can almost hear an audible sigh escape His lips, see Him raise a frustrated hand to His forehead, slowly working it down His face and off the tip of His beard. Then He motioned the father to bring the boy forward. *Come here.* Immediately, He healed the young man of his condition.

Let's watch now the leadership style of Jesus. You can imagine His frustrated disciples. Here they'd stepped up to try doing something that, honestly, yes, they'd been a little afraid to attempt. They weren't sure they knew how to do it. And as everyone could plainly see by now—they'd failed at it. They'd been unable to figure out what words they were supposed to say, what order they were supposed to say them in, the way they were supposed to hold their mouths or whatever, to perform the job that everyone expected them to perform.

I'd guess the temptation at this point to quit altogether was fairly high—just forget trying to pretend they belonged on this team that Jesus had put together, these men He had called to follow Him. Why not go back to doing what they'd been doing beforehand, back to the kind of life and lifestyle they felt more qualified to lead, the things they already knew they were pretty good at? Let somebody else do this.

Instead, they did something important and worth noticing. They went to Jesus "in private" (v. 19). They got alone with Him, the way we get alone with Him when we come to Him in prayer. And they asked Him for help. They asked to understand. They brought their not-knowing-how to the feet of Jesus and basically asked, "Why weren't we able to do that?" (see v. 19).

His answer, in verse 20, is vitally instructive. Not only to them but also to us. He didn't focus on the flaws in their technique. He didn't break down their performance and criticize them for the steps they missed. The surface details weren't the issue. They rarely are. Instead, He saved His word of counsel, not for an analysis of what they'd already done and tried and not known how to do but, rather, for what would set them up for success in the future as they went back out there and tried again.

The answer—the crux of Jesus' answer—was *faith*. "I tell you, if you have faith as small as a mustard seed, you can say to this mountain, 'Move from here to there,' and it will move. Nothing will be impossible for you" (v. 20).

And, friend, I see no reason why the implications of this well-known biblical theme wouldn't apply to us, or why they wouldn't apply to how we lead our family spiritually. The secret is never going to come from simply following instructions in a book or trying to pacify your spouse's expectations of you or copying what somebody else in your church or small group is doing. The bottom-line ingredient is simply faith. Faith in Christ's *sufficiency*.

Sure, you're going to come up against some challenges. All of us do. You're going to feel a little uncomfortable sometimes, exposed, vulnerable. You won't like it when there's not as much enthusiasm as you'd hoped around the table, when you're needing to be the one who—perhaps all alone, unilaterally—is having to champion the importance of what you're doing. You'll be exhausted at times by how many obstacles the Enemy will introduce into your own life and into your family's life, anything to divert and detour you away from steadily following the path you believe you've been led to walk. But remember what the apostle Peter said, after describing the Devil as prowling "around like a roaring lion looking for someone to devour." He told us to "resist him," standing firm in our, what?—our *faith*— "because you know that the family of believers throughout the world is undergoing the same kind of sufferings" (1 Peter 5:8–9).

The answer is always faith. Faith in Christ's sufficiency.

WHO'S ON FIRST?

Oftentimes when we start thinking about stepping up into this place of spiritual leadership, taking responsibility for the vision and direction of our homes, the priority shift we feel called to make is to finally start putting our family first. We might say, *my wife*—I haven't been loving her well or listening to her well or appreciating her as I should. *My kids*—I haven't been spending enough time with them, haven't been paying them enough attention, haven't been making sure they know how much I love them, how proud I am of them. All of that is key to moving in the right direction. If you're like most people, there's a good chance you could stand some improvement in those areas.

The primary change that's needed in pursuing a more focused kind of leadership at home, however, is not, as you might think, putting your family first. *Family*, as odd as the following statement may sound, is just as capable of becoming an idol in your life as any of the other idols you've created, whether work, money, television, deer hunting season, or more specific sin areas—anything to which you yield your supreme loyalty and allegiance. You may need to put family *higher* on the priority list. That would probably be a good move. But putting them first? No. Only God comes first.

I was working for Coca-Cola when a Christian friend of mine drew a little diagram for me that fundamentally changed how I thought about my job, my family, my life, my everything. On a piece of paper he sketched two identical grids containing four blank, horizontal lines, each in descending order, and then he asked me a series of fairly simple questions.

"Who is the owner of your company?"

"Coca-Cola."

"Who is your employer? To whom do you answer?"

"The CEO."

"Who is the employee?"

"Me. I am."

"Who is your customer?"

"Uh, people who buy Coke?"

"No."

Leaving that marked-up grid alone, he moved on to the next one. But he gave me a new starting point for filling this one out. "Secular company, sacred company, it doesn't really matter," he said. "The way for a Christian to view the hierarchy of any organization is to see that *God*, in reality, is the Owner of it. He's the One who occupies that top spot." The company name didn't go at the top of this grid. Write God's name in there instead.

My friend went on: "All right. And yet even with God as the Owner of the company, you still answer to the same person, the same employer, right? And you, of course, are still the employee. But think—who's your customer?"

Hmm. The answer, I now realized, was probably not everybody on the planet who drank Coca-Cola products. That was more of a task than God, as the Owner, would give to any one person. Nowhere in any kind of board meeting or morale-building exercise—if *God* was the company owner—would He imply that *my job* was to get the whole world drinking Coke. I can't do that. But as is wisely said in certain business circles, "It's always about the people; it's never about the shingle." And the people, in my case, on whom I could exert the most direct influence, were the national account sales reps who answered to me. *They* were my real customer. Invest in *them*, pour into *them*, and guess what—I'd be part of creating an environment where more people could drink more Coke in more places around the world. I'd be doing my job. By putting God first. And by knowing my customer.

But I can't serve my customer well by just doing whatever they want me to do, by playing whatever role they want me to play. By putting *them* first. They're not in charge of framing policy and driving the ship. Their whims are not my commands. They're important to me, yes—*vitally* important. Invaluably important. I care deeply about them, and I would do anything in the world for them. I listen to them, and I take their concerns and suggestions under full consideration. But what they mostly need from me is to be guided wisely with specific strategies and information that's coming down to me from above me, from leadership, from ownership.

Watch how this same concept translates from work to family. If everything is starting with the Owner and His priorities, which are shared with me as I spend time listening to Him and learning from Him, and then flowing through me from His sufficiency, equipping me to guide and direct and communicate and motivate my family by my faith in the One who's guiding and directing *me*, then I can hardly say I'm on my own to figure out what to do and how to do it. The One who is most invested in this enterprise—God, the Owner—will always make sure that I, the mere steward of this task, am well-equipped to take care of His (and my) customer so He can carry out His larger kingdom work through all of us.

We're in good hands, people. This Owner of ours is the ultimate example of one whose company is "too big to fail." And He has said that "nothing will be impossible" for employees like us, whose faith may be only the size of a grape nut, but it's sufficient—through *His* sufficiency—to accomplish what He wants to see happen.

LET IT HAPPEN

I hope I've been able to persuade you of the necessity for writing down your plan and then keeping yourself accountable to it. Now, I don't mean that by writing down your plan you can never budge or adjust or speed up or slow down. And I don't mean that by being accountable you and your family engage in an overbearing type of scrutiny, becoming hall monitors, but mainly that an encouraging, helpful, uplifting brand of accountability can help everybody see the value in reaching individual goals and working together.

But even with a written plan that we keep subject to healthy accountability, you and I can still be susceptible to fear of failure. With all the physical safeguards in place, we can find ourselves under dark clouds, such as guilt, inadequacy, discouragement, fatigue, rejection, inconsistency, you name it.

Most of these phantoms, I've found, are the residue left over from trying to be the man. From trying to be the one on whom everything is dependent. And here's why that's a problem: the gospel, try as we might to insert even an ounce of personal effort and entitlement into it, is in all ways a God-thing. All of it. He creates; He compels; He loves; He saves. He just does it. Jesus did it. He's made a covenant. He keeps it. While I realize our faith and obedience roll up into it and affect the dynamic, day to day, He is not counting on *you* for a successful outcome, either of your life or your life plan. He is fully confident in Himself of keeping His promises to you and sustaining you through every up and down. You have a responsibility, yes, but you are not ultimately responsible.

This reality I've just described is meant to be *freeing* to us, not frustrating. It's meant to lift *off* the discouragement and downheartedness, not pile it on. But whenever we look to other people for our inspiration and means of comparison, whenever we think we ourselves are the ones who should always know what to do, always able to do it better/faster/stronger, whenever our theological conclusions about human capabilities come anywhere close to nudging out our need for Christ's full sufficiency, that's when we're sitting ducks for things like inadequacy, discouragement, inconsistency, all of that.

The more I read and study the Bible, the more I'm left with a high view of God and a much lower, much more realistic view of man. We are made in His image, of course. We've been imbued with significant value, greater than any other beings He created. But we are fallen sinners without a single buttonhole or bootstrap. We cannot pull ourselves up. We are thoroughly dependent on God coming down.

But this is not a point of weakness. Instead, it's our gateway to magnificent strength. To direction, purpose, and spiritual confidence. To invigorating insight and energy.

Nobody's expecting you to be perfect at this undertaking. No one's sizing up your shoulder measurements for the Superman or Superwoman cape. Anyone who's looking to you as the source of their sufficiency is, as you well know, sure to be sadly disappointed. But not if they know where *your* sufficiency is coming from. Not if that four-piece assortment of surrender, sacrifice, humility, and dependence is constantly working, baking into your heart, until it's less descriptive of your goals and simply more descriptive of your character.

That's what will start to happen when your beginning point each day is the cross of Christ, the place where your sufficiency was fought for and won. Instead of guilt, *forgiveness*. Instead of inadequacy, *power*. Instead of discouragement, *hope*. Instead of fatigue, *endurance*. Instead of rejection, *acceptance*. Instead of inconsistency, *faithfulness*.

Resolve and perseverance. Discernment and sensitivity. Along with the much more regular appearance of joy. All because of your faith in Christ's sufficiency.

CHAPTER 14

LEGACY

I kept seeing this vision.

Now, I'm not a guy who sees visions. *Vision*, I like. *Vision*, I can do. But *visions*—plural—those weren't the kind of experiences I was accustomed to having. Yet fairly often, during those early days of this renaissance period in my life, when I would be quietly praying, asking God to show me His will and desire in leading my family, asking Him to please use me for the purpose He'd called me to serve, I would get this image in my mind of people, like a long line of stick people, stretching back as far as the eye could see. A winding road, filled with people, multitudes of people, rounding over distant rises in the terrain. One after another. People.

It bothered me. I really wasn't sure what I was seeing. But I'm just telling you, it was there. In my mind. Most of the time. During prayer. And I kept wondering, *What does this mean? Why am I seeing this? What am I supposed to be taking from it?*

I went to one of the men who routinely has been helpful to me in thinking through and processing my life with Christ, someone who really knows the Word, and I told him what I'd been experiencing. I asked him, "What do you think is happening here?"

So he took me to Revelation 7, which (I've come to realize later) is connected to the apostle John's prior vision in Revelation 5, where God is pictured sitting on a throne, surrounded by the elders and angels, holding in His hand an unopened scroll. John begins to weep because no one is able to open the scroll and see what's written on it. But at that moment a Lamb appears at the center of the throne room—the crucified and risen Christ—the One who with His blood has purchased the souls of the redeemed "from every tribe and language and people and nation" (Rev. 5:9). And in Revelation 7, verse 14, here they come.

"They're coming out of the Tribulation," my friend explained as he read. "They've 'washed their robes and made them white in the blood of the Lamb.' And now they're standing before the throne, worshiping God, preparing to spend all eternity with Him. 'Never again will they hunger; never again will they thirst' (v. 16). The Lamb will be their Shepherd, supplying them with everything they need, forever and ever. 'And God will wipe away every tear from their eyes' (v. 17)."

That was it. That's what God had been showing me. As I listened to what the Bible said, confirmed by what my friend and mentor said, I interpreted this vision as meaning that God's desire for me—in fact, for *all* of us—was to be personally involved in this massive influx of people coming into the kingdom by introducing as many of them as possible to the gospel, by introducing them to Christ.

Everyone is looking for a champion. Everyone wants a way of life that satisfies and completes them. And the only Champion, the only choice, is the One who emanates from the center of that throne room in heaven. That's where we are going by God's grace, by our faith in the Lamb. That's where whatever influence we've been given as believers should be most keenly directed as we live out the balance of each day, days that will go on to become the balance of our lives.

We can spend our days and years on earth pursuing other goals and dreams, chasing other visions. But what could possibly be more important than this one task, this one mission? Saving people for eternity is not our responsibility, but sharing the gospel, living the gospel, being shaped by the gospel, being transformed heart and soul by the gospel—*this* is our responsibility. Our privilege. Our honor. Our legacy.

What God has shown me in the many years since those days is that by far—*by far!*—my most direct route to fulfilling this enormous calling of mine (and ours) is to live it and share it and instill it within those who are closest to me: *my family.* They are the essential starting point where any hope of my being effective, any hope of becoming my very best for the kingdom, must begin. By myself, I may be able to touch only a small number of people's lives for Christ, a small circle within a confined number of years. But through *them*—through my children—this number multiplies significantly. And through the generations? Just think about it. That number simply explodes.

That is how legacy is built.

ACROSS THE MILES, ACROSS THE YEARS

I received an unusual and unexpected text from my daughter one evening. She was sitting in a Bible study at her church in

Minnesota, where the person leading the session that night had raised the question about what happens to us after we die and was attempting to answer it.

Interestingly enough, we'd been talking about this very subject not long beforehand during one of our Sunday night family phone calls. And as my daughter sat there listening to the man's explanations and presuppositions, she felt pretty sure that some of what he was saying was not biblically accurate. She couldn't exactly put her finger on the verse we'd been studying that spoke about it, so she'd been sort of flipping through the Bible in her lap, seeking to locate it. But being able to recall only a snippet of it—the gist—she decided to text me from her seat in the class.

"Dad," her message said, "this guy says our bodies basically go to sleep when we die, that we don't go immediately to heaven. Is that true?"

Well, again, let me clarify: I don't know how long I could last in a serious theological debate and be able to sway anyone's opinion or belief. I'm largely self-taught—Holy Spirit–taught—in addition to what I've learned from the pulpit and from various Bible study groups and leaders. But I did immediately think of at least one verse—probably the same one *you're* thinking of—where Paul talked about being "away from the body and at home with the Lord." Grabbing my Bible, I confirmed what the verse said, then shot my daughter back a reply message: "Look at 2 Corinthians 5:8."

While waiting for her follow-up text to arrive, I scanned the first part of that chapter, where Paul reiterated how, when our "earthly tent" is destroyed, we have an "eternal house in heaven"—how we are "swallowed up by life" and made safe in our "heavenly dwelling" (vv. 1, 4). Tracing some of the cross-references from that passage into other books and chapters of the Bible, I found Philippians 1:23—Paul, writing from prison, where he wasn't certain he would survive his time of confinement, saying, "I desire to depart and be with Christ, which is better by far." I found John 12:26 also—Jesus predicting His upcoming death, encouraging His followers to persevere but saying that even if their faith should cost them their lives, they could be confident knowing "where I am, my servant also will be."

So I started firing verses back at her. "Ask him this," I said. "Ask him how he explains this verse." "Here's another Scripture." "Ask him this."

I wasn't there in the room, of course. I was at home in Georgia. But knowing my daughter the way I do, I could see her raising her hand. I could hear her commenting, "Hey, my dad is responding to me, and he's saying . . ."

To say the least, we were shaking up the Bible study teacher.

But that's not really the point of my story, nor was this my reason for getting involved. The part I like best is what happened afterward, when several people came up to my daughter and said, "Man, that was amazing. Is your dad a pastor?"

"No." She laughed. "We just study the Bible together as a family. And I happened to remember that we'd spent some time looking at this subject recently." The chance for her to be able to inspire others with how God has inspired us to stay rooted in His Word—I just hope several people walked out of church that night thinking, *I want to do that with my kids too.*

It's a little taste of legacy.

But my favorite story from that evening was the one she told of a woman who approached her afterward and said, "I just want to thank you for being able to shed that insight for us tonight.

My grandfather passed away a couple of weeks ago, and my understanding had been that, as a Christian, he's in heaven right now. I've drawn a lot of comfort from that. But when I heard this thing tonight, you know, about how he's just asleep or in limbo or whatever—that he's not even *in* heaven—he was all I could think about, like, 'Well, where *is* he, then?' So I'm just really thankful for you and your father, for helping me see what the Bible says about it."

Remember me sharing in the previous chapter about having a high view of God? Having a big-God theology? This is the kind of theology I hold because that's what I believe the Bible teaches. But I also believe it because of moments like these. Moments when I'm doing absolutely nothing other than the equivalent of what I was doing that night—sitting at home, minding my own business. Yet God—through my children and through experiences that flow from His long-ago calling to create a plan for their spiritual growth—remains hard at work. Through us. Through them.

I mean, how else can you explain how this plan could possibly, in our wildest dreams, impact a young woman in Minnesota, grieving over the loss of a dear relative, being encouraged in her faith by what the Bible says about God's promises to her? Mere mortals can't pull off that kind of thing.

So this tells me something crucially important to remember. None of us, when motivated by the Lord to craft a family discipleship plan, can actually even *begin* to plan for what He's already placed in motion—plans to touch a world far beyond the raw square footage of our homes.

But that's the God who's directing you—a big God who chooses to do big things through His people. And with a God like this behind you, above you, underneath you, and surrounding you, your legacy is sure to be much, much bigger than you realize.

So please, if at any point you've felt yourself lost in the high weeds of what we've been discussing—if even right now your overwhelming feeling is the feeling of being overwhelmed, and if at any point in the future, as you put prayer and pencil to paper, you become discouraged—for whatever reason that may come along to stall your momentum for continuing to keep going, hear me. You are not doing this alone. Any weight or pressure you feel (if you indeed feel any weight or pressure) is not yours to handle all by yourself. That's because the weight of your plan's influence is resting squarely on the broad, capable shoulders of almighty God. And He is 100 percent *sufficient* (to repeat one of my two favorite words) to translate this plan of yours into a hundred years or more of (my other favorite word) *legacy*.

LAST WORDS

Thank you so much for hanging with me this whole way, for pushing forward to the very end. I am praying daily for you and for other readers just like you, that God will supply everything needed to help put wings on your desire to make Christ known to your children.

In our last few moments together, I want to sum up how I feel about the importance of this plan and give you a final word of encouragement—but I'm fishing for a word a little bit stronger than that—to press into this process and allow God to make huge changes in the course of your family's future.

Almost all of us possess some kind of mental, visual image for where we want our families to go. I hope as you've been reading that nothing has made you feel bad or has washed over you with guilt for not having done more to solidify those images into a workable form. But plans and images that we keep in our heads die with us. And all we leave behind to go forward is one generation's worth of memories. We know from Israel's experience after the death of Joshua, if from nothing else, exactly how long it can potentially take for those memories to stop speaking at all.

Paper plans, however, live on.

The only reason I was able to learn about the Christian faith that existed generations before me in my family line was through the written records of those who documented their prayers, their thoughts, and their experiences with God. When I am the long-gone great-great-great-grandfather of what could be a large number of great-great-great-grandchildren, I want them to be handed and shown and taught some version of a plan that God initiated in my life—a plan designed not only for my *immediate* children's benefit but also for theirs. I want their early awareness of God to be that of a heavenly Father who loves them so much that He instructed one of their distant relatives, a hundred or more years before, to prepare something for them that could bless their lives every single day.

That's why I've written down our plan. I singularly refuse for a succeeding generation in my family to grow up "who knew neither the LORD nor what he had done for Israel" (Judg. 2:10)—or for the Chatmons—not if I have anything to do with it.

So when my children, upon my death, receive the particulars of my last will and testament (and I know they'll be there to hear it because they'll know a cash payout is involved), they also will be given from my folder of final documents a reading of our family's Blue Sheet plan. It's right there today among my important, official papers. As their legacy. Because this is real to me. It's that important.

I recognize, according to the latest statistics, a little more than half of all American adults don't have a will of any sort, haven't made any kind of estate plan or written down their wishes for how to handle the distribution of their assets. The main reason, besides perhaps the morbidity of contemplating one's own death, is the expectation that making a will is too complex and confusing of a process. In the same way that an estate plan needn't be the size of a Supreme Court decision in order to be effective and put into force, neither does your plan for family discipleship have to be anything fancy and sophisticated. It just needs to be you and your faith and your family vision on paper. In order for it to survive beyond your lifetime, you do have to write it out. You need a written plan.

God can do anything, of course, with anybody, with any family. But for our part, we will not do what we don't plan to do. When we don't *plan* for God to work in our family's lives, we unwittingly stand in the way of His blessings. If we *do* plan, however, He puts us in a position to experience the most breathtaking blessing of all.

I actually, to be completely honest and forthcoming, have experienced one other kind of vision in my life, in addition to the one I described at the outset of this chapter. It's similar but incredibly personal. It's a scene I can describe only as a "Welcoming Committee." In this mental image, I foresee the future generations of my family coming into heaven, one by one, robed in white. My children. My grandchildren. My great-grandchildren. Stepping into heaven to be received by Christ their Savior. But they also will be received by me—as well as by others. Such as my father, grandfather, and great-grandfather. And all the others who represent *my* Welcoming Committee when I arrive under the blood of the Lamb in the realms of eternal glory.

Because of God's common grace to all mankind, as well as His covenant grace toward those who receive Him as Lord, our life on earth—despite its unavoidable difficulties—affords us many opportunities for experiencing His blessing, for feeling pleasure, for knowing what it means to be happy, to sense joy. But I can think of no joy more abundant—more buckling at the knees—than the sheer rush of holy adrenaline that a redeemed, resurrected body must feel when his or her own child, or the children of their children, steps into the presence of God in preparation for an eternity of life with Him.

These are not stick people to us. These are our own flesh and blood. While they join in that long line of the redeemed, coming out of the "tribulation" known as life on a fallen planet—and while our relationships with our children will surely be transformed in heaven into something even greater than the intimacy of home and family here on earth—the blessing of enjoying eternity with them as fellow sons and daughters of God, as heirs of Christ's bounty, is more than words can describe.

But by making Christ known to our kids, by creating an environment where they can explore and experience Him in everyday ways, and by trusting Him to work in their lives as only this big God who made them and loves them can do it, we get to pursue the prize to which we as parents were created and called.

Legacy.

GENERATIONAL SPIRITUAL DEVELOPMENT PLAN

CREATED FOR _____

COMMITMENT DATE _____

MAP IT OUT!

To equip and encourage your family to design a Christ-centered spiritual plan, spend time with your spouse and your age-appropriate children to prayerfully consider your responses to the following questions that represent the five key areas of concern:

1. *Vision*
2. *Mission*
3. *Values*
4. *Goals*
5. *Prayer*

1. Vision: What You Are Attempting to Accomplish

To develop your vision, you need to recall your own personal story and explore why you believe faith and a relationship with God are important for your family.

Write your personal testimony of coming to Christ.

Why is faith an essential element for your family now and in generations to come?

2. Mission: How You Will Accomplish It

Your mission is how you will live out your vision. Determine the ones you are trusting for your spiritual maturity and salvation and what processes you might use to live out your life of faith in your family and in the world around you.

Who is your source for direction and guidance?

How will you develop a spiritual core and framework for your family to follow?

3. Values: Your Nonnegotiable Core Beliefs

Your values drive your decisions. Think about what you believe, value, and consider to be nonnegotiable priorities in your personal and family life.

List up to ten values you desire you and your family to have.

• _____

• _____

• _____

- _____

- _____

- _____

- _____

- _____

- _____

- _____

- _____

4. Goals: What Moves You Closer to Realizing Your Vision

Read Ephesians 6:4, Proverbs 22:15, and Deuteronomy 6:4–9 to help determine three things you can do this year to train and instruct your children in the Lord.

Set no more than three goals per year for your family.

What are some goals that will focus your family on how to demonstrate the Word of God?

What are some goals that will equip and encourage your family to stand firm in their beliefs and be Christ-centered?

What are some goals that will equip and encourage them to share the hope they have or are learning to have in Christ?

- _____

- _____

- _____

5. Prayer: The Power Behind the Plan

Intercessory prayer is the key to success. As you pray, God will provide wisdom, direction, inspiration, and encouragement as you develop and live out your family's Generational Spiritual Development Plan.

How can you pray specifically for your family?

What do you want to teach your children about prayer (see James 5:16)?

FAMILY INFORMATION

List the members of your family, and complete the data boxes to include their roles in the family, where they are in their spiritual journeys—whether Christian or Decision Pending—and whether they have shared their personal testimonies of coming to faith in Christ with the family.

APPENDIX A

NAME	ROLE IN FAMILY	SPIRITUAL JOURNEY	SHARED TESTIMONY
Terence Chatmon	Father	Christian	Yes

APPENDIX B

SAMPLE DEVOTIONAL PLAN

THEME: YEAR OF CONNECTION (KNOWING WHO GOD IS AND YOUR RELATIONSHIP WITH HIM)

- What do we really believe?
- Whom do we follow?
- Why do we believe what we say we believe?
- How do we come to know Him intimately?
- Whom do we know and feel compelled to serve?

SCRIPTURES

And Jesus came and said to them, "All authority in heaven and on earth has been given to me. Go therefore and make disciples of all nations, baptizing them in the name of the Father and of the Son and of the Holy Spirit, teaching them to observe all that I have commanded you. And behold, I am with you always, to the end of the age." (Matthew 28:18–20 ESV)

Jesus answered, "I am the way and the truth and the life. No one comes to the Father except through me. If you really know me, you will know my Father as well." (John 14:6–7)

"Call to me and I will answer you and tell you great and unsearchable things you do not know." (Jeremiah 33:3)

FAMILY VISION STATEMENT: UNITY IN THE SPIRIT

GENERATIONS UPON GENERATIONS KNOWING WHO CHRIST IS AND HAVING GREAT DELIGHT IN A LIFE OF PRAYER, WORSHIP, AND LEARNING WHO GOD IS AND WHAT HE HAS DONE.

FAMILY MISSION STATEMENT: PLANT THE PLAN, PLANT THE WORD, PLANT THE LEGACY

TO EQUIP AND ENCOURAGE THE FAMILY TO EMBRACE THE PRINCIPLES OF CHRISTIAN BIBLICAL TRUTHS AND CHRIST-CENTERED VALUES SO THAT THE FAMILY WILL LIVE A LIFE OF OUTREACH (WITNESSING) AND A LIFE WORTHY OF THE CALLING.

GOALS: A DESCRIPTION OF WHAT WE ARE TO BE, TO DO, OR TO GET

By the end of this year, we should understand why we believe what we believe and be able to share and defend our faith to others. We will have a greater understanding of what it means to know the Father, Jesus Christ, and the Holy Spirit. To accomplish this, our three specific goals for this year are:

1. To study the gospel of John.
2. To participate in or complete a study on apologetics.
3. To be able to say chronologically the sixty-six books of the Bible.

CHATMON DEVOTIONAL PLAN: YEAR OF CONNECTION

It is my prayer that we will grow stronger in our faith this year and will memorize a favorite Bible verse from this year's readings.

DATE	TOPIC	OPENING PRAYER	LEAD (TEACHER)
1/5	A Time for Prayer	Wanda	Terence
1/19	A Time for Prayer	Danielle	Wanda
2/2	A Time for Prayer	Shannon	Torry
2/16	John 1	Torry	Terence
3/2	John 2	Terence	Shannon
3/16	John 3	Wanda	Terence
3/30	John 4	Terence	Wanda

4/13	John 5	Shannon	Danielle
4/27	John 6	Torry	Shannon
5/11	John 7	Terence	Torry
5/25	John 8	Wanda	Terence
6/8	John 9	Terence	Wanda
6/22	John 10	All	All
7/13	John 11	Torry	Danielle
7/27	John 12	Danielle	All
8/10	John 13	Shannon	Torry
8/24	John 14	Danielle	Shannon
9/7	John 15	Terence	Wanda
9/14	John 16	Wanda	Terence
10/5	John 17	Terence	Danielle
10/19	John 18	All	All
11/2	John 19	Danielle	Wanda
11/16	John 20	Torry	Danielle
11/30	John 21	Shannon	Torry
12/14	Recap the book of John	Wanda	Terence
12/25	Celebration: Christmas Dinner	All	All

Meditate On All Year

The unwanted will of God is good, if you believe that God is good.

Daily Prayer

Lord, we come to You with adoration and thanksgiving. We ask You to grant us today the desire to seek Your authentic glory, by means of grace alone, according to the truth of Your Word. Amen.

ABOUT THE AUTHOR

*T*erence Chatmon, a successful senior executive in corporate America, served in leadership roles with several Fortune 50 companies, including Johnson & Johnson, Citibank, and Coca-Cola, but was failing to become the spiritual leader of his home. Challenged by his wife to chart a course for the spiritual growth of his family and children, Terence took what he knew from his corporate-world success and biblical teaching to develop, with much prayer, one of the world's most transformational step-by-step family spiritual development processes.

Terence is now a family legacy champion, and his family discipleship workshop, Charting Your Family's Spiritual Course, has reached more than twenty thousand participating families and continues to grow. He is also the president and CEO of Fellowship of Companies for Christ International (FCCI.org), a network of executive leaders spanning more than one hundred countries. FCCI uses training conferences, personal relationships, and a rich library of resources to equip and encourage business leaders to see their companies and careers as powerful tools for transformational change.

A Chicago native and graduate of the University of Illinois, Terence brings drive and ingenuity to every role he plays in life, as an elder at a prominent eight-thousand-member megachurch, a Bible study teacher, and, most important, a husband and father.